Slam's Dirty Boxing for the Street

Destructive Tools, Tips, Techniques & Strategies

Randall Slamowitz

SLAM'S DIRTY BOXING FOR THE STREET

DESTRUCTIVE TOOLS, TIPS, TECHNIQUES & STRATEGIES

By Randall Slamowitz

Table of Contents

Dedication

This book is dedicated to all the previous mentors that I have followed and learned from over the past 40 years of training. I have learned many things from the traditional arts, as well as the combative side. I still consider myself a life-long student, and I always keep an open mind to continually learn, adapt and grow my skills and knowledge.

I want to give a very special dedication to all my students, past and present that have trusted my guidance. I hope that I have made a difference in their lives to be better than they were before.

I would like to thank and acknowledge my current students for being good ukes and helping me with the photos in this book.

Chris Warren-Uke
John Harrington-Uke,
Kamal Southall- Photographer
Ashley Martin-Uke

Introduction

Through the years I have gathered an extensive amount of information that is always floating around in my head or scattered in piles of notes around my office, which have not been filed. My students have been telling me for years to write a book because memory will only last so long. I finally decided to write it down in formal order. This book will be my first attempt to pass on at least some culmination of my 40 years of gained knowledge with a realistic, no-nonsense approach.

My intention for writing this is to give you what I perceive to be the most realistic set of ideas, tools, tips, strategies, techniques, as well as mind-set. Some things you might already know but, I am certain that there will be something in here that you haven't seen, tried, or thought about. I always tell my students, if there is something that you do not like, or are not comfortable with....don't use it. Being a firm believer that martial arts isn't a cookie cutter endeavor, I try to incorporate tools, strategies, and techniques that can be applied to each individual. After all, we each have different builds, weights, attributes, strengths, and weaknesses What is a good technique for a short person may not be good for a tall one.

However, I must stress that there are no such magical techniques or strikes that will help you be invincible. If you are looking for that ancient secret, it does not exist. This book will help tip the odds in your favor if you read, absorb the information, and train. Nothing takes the place of training.

I must start out by saying that this book is not intended for the newbie in mind. You should at least have an idea of basic boxing. This is additional information to add to your basic boxing skills. Therefore I am not going to go into detail on the basics as far as (8 count punches and basic movement). There are lots of videos and other books that cover them in great detail. The focus of this book is on adding unorthodox strikes and ideas that go beyond the norm for street encounters.

Disclaimers

"There is nothing new under the sun." I want to mention that as much as I would love to take the credit for any of the tools or techniques in this book, they are not my original thoughts to claim. My arrangements and ways of using them is my own take, and reason for writing this book.

Note: I have names and terms for techniques and tools that in different arts and styles etc. may be called something different.

For the sake of variation, I am using the terms aggressor, attacker, opponent and him interchangeably to signify the same thing.

Your brain is the weapon-
Everything else is considered a tool.

Principles and Tactics to Win:

Use the Element of surprise and Deception to your Advantage
Catch you aggressor off guard to make first contact.

Strike Preemptively
Strike first, strike fast and strike hard.

Closest Weapon to the Nearest Target
Meaning your closest weapon might be your front hand to his nearest target might be his face. The shortest line of fire is the fastest.

Get Off the Line of Attack
For straight attacks get off line. Use angles when possible. Shift the head and the body off the line of attack.

Feinting
Fake set-up a punch or kick to have your opponent react such as attempting to finger jab at the eye or a low oblique kick to the shin to take the opponent's mind off the real attack.

High -Low
This principle means aiming and alternating punches and kicks to the high line and to the low line at different targets on the attacker's body which keeps him at least a step behind the curve by having to guess/react to what is being thrown at them. Putting him in defensive mode.

Flanking
Going around or to the side. Not going through "No Mans' Land", but around it. This can be a good strategic plan. When you are squared off with an opponent you are facing all his tools (8 limbs) and a head. If you flank you automatically cut his arsenal in at least half. Plus, you have good strategic positioning to take his back. Your hips should be perpendicular to your opponent.

Crashing
Taking opponent's space. Taking an opponent's space is a Silat concept to unbalance a person. Take your opponent's space he will have nowhere to stand, will not have a good base, and be unbalanced. If unbalanced he can't fight – too busy trying not to fall.

Mind set:
"Wherever you are, you are standing in my space"– Joseph Simonet

Forward Pressure
Keeps opponent off balance and back pedaling on his heels. If he is on his heels he is off balance and cannot strike because he is trying to catch himself from falling.

Attack Vital Targets - Eyes Throat, Groin, Solar Plexus, Jaw Line, Brachial Plexus.

Control Distance/Range - Control the range that you want to fight in. Control distance and make it work for you.

Keep your Hands Up and Stay Covered- Always be conscious of being covered, even when attacking.

Branching- If a strike is not getting through or is not causing damage because the area is now covered. Don't waste time striking it. Attack a different area.

Take their Balance- Take their balance and they will be too busy trying not to fall. Even if they managed to get a strike off it would have no power behind it. If you have no base, you have no stability which means no power.

Take their Breathing- Knock the wind out of them and they won't be able to fight.

Take their Vision- Take his sight and he can't see to fight.

Take their Consciousness- Shake the brain/Shut the main computer down.

Quick Definition on Combat/Mind-set
Martial Arts is what you do *with* somebody. Combatives is what you do *to* somebody.

A fight is 90% attitude and 10% physical!

This is my favorite quote that I think applies...

"It's not the size of the dog in the fight, it's the size of the fight in the dog!"
– Mark Twain

"Empty your mind, be formless. Shapeless, like water. If you put water into a cup, it becomes the cup. You put water into a bottle and it becomes the bottle. You put it in a teapot, it becomes the teapot. Now, water can flow or it can crash. Be water, my friend."
– Bruce Lee

The Stance

Basic Fighting Stance is roughly heel to toe. Feet are about shoulder width a part. Knees slightly bent. Chin down looking under your brow, teeth clinched, and shoulders up, "Nose over toes" – Do not lean too forward or lean too far back. Balance and maneuverability are the keys Your hands are up. The rear hand touches your cheek or temple. The front up by your cheek and face, but out about 6-12 inches. Front foot and knee are slightly inward. This is to protect your groin. Have the heel of your rear foot up ready to spring off of. This is an athletic stance, and you should be relaxed and loose. If you are too tight or tense, you will not move quickly.

Basic Index Position: The Stand Off

This position should always be used during a confrontation. You are basically in the boxing stance with your hands open and extended to show that you have no intention of being aggressive to your attacker or on-lookers. Geoff Thompson coined the phrase "**Fence**" Your hands are creating an Invisible fence between you and you aggressor. Your stance should be non-aggressive, but athletic and ready to spring into action.

Hands should be up and open by your face. Your main areas that you want to protect in a physical altercation are your jaw and neck. Getting hit on the jaw line or chin could be a knockout blow and should be protected in case of punches. In case a sharp object is presented your neck should be protected. Therefore, the hands are kept up.

Fence Stance Side view facing aggressor.

TIP:
It is better if your hands are above your aggressor's. This is similar to the analogy of trying to get your hands on the top of a baseball bat. The winner's hand is on top.

Jedi Mind TIP:
Keep you open hands staggered in the center at your aggressor. By doing this you are subconsciously leading or telling your aggressor where to throw his punches so you can be ready with the appropriate response. Keeping your hands up to the center closes off the path for throwing straight punches because your hands will be in the way. The only avenue left is to swing around the barrier making him throw rounded punches.

Fence Stance Front view
With my hands splayed open I seem to look non aggressive. But notice that I am basically in a boxing stance. All I have to do is close my open hands into fists. My hands and arms are high enough to cover my face if something is thrown at me.

Distancing

While getting into your fence position, your rear foot should take a step back to create distance between you and your aggressor. Creating distance will give you more time to react. **Distance = More time to react**.

No Mans' Land

The space or distancing between two people that are squaring off I refer to as "**No Mans' Land**". It is the space, or the gap that if you step into you will be close enough to be hit by the other person. To make contact with the other person you usually must take a step into "No Mans' Land". There are several strategic ways to go about doing this without the painful consequences of being hit. This is referred to as "closing the gap" in sparring. The goal is to stay outside of "**No Mans' Land**", which is out of the opponent's reach until you are ready to attack.

Where to Look

Since we have made our space we should be able to take in the whole body of our aggressor. My take is that your main focus should be the center of his chest. However, I am visually looking at the whole body, his arms, fists and legs. Anything that can reach out and hit me. It is possible to see a dip or movement in the shoulders when the aggressor is ready to throw something at you. I am not staring at his face or his eyes. After-all his face isn't what will hit you. It will be one of his extremities. The eyes can give false information as to what your opponent will do.

TIP:
Peripheral vision is quicker than looking directly.
You should be able to look straight at your attacker's chest and also out of the corners of your eyes at the same time.
With your peripheral vision you should see the rest of his body.
When he moves you should be able to pick it up right away.

Boxing Stance for the Street

I want to mention that a boxing stance for the street is a little different than in the ring. Hands should always be kept up to cover the head. The rear hand should be covering the jaw line, or it can go up to the temple. In sport you can lower your hands and open your stance. If you get hit your opponent is wearing gloves and there is a ref to stop the fight or intervene. On the street you do not have that luxury. If you get hit or knocked out. It could mean your life vs losing a match and coming back to have a rematch another day.

I am tight to make as small a target as possible. My chin is down, shoulders up and teeth are clinched. I am looking out just under my brow. My knees are slightly bent like a spring and my rear heal is slightly raised to burst or explode if needed.

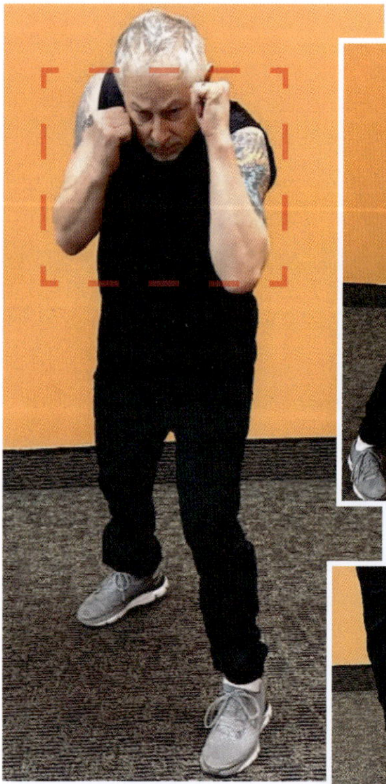

Front View

Side Views

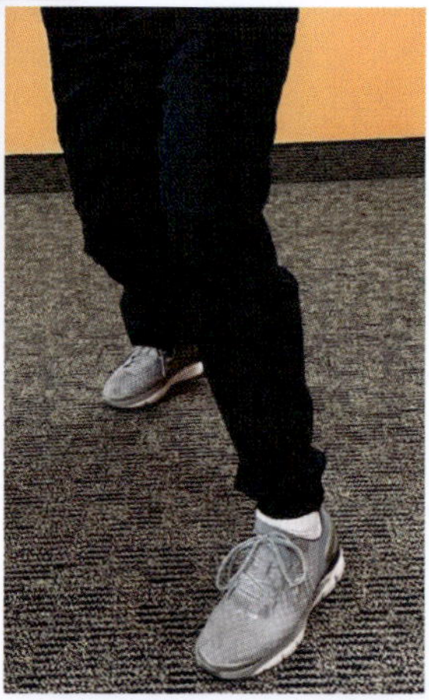

Note:

Some of the things that you start to consider in the street that are not neccessarily thought about in sport is a kick to the groin.

For that reason I keep my foot and my knee inward which is a more closed stance than in sport.

False Lead

A deceptive stance that is used in the Filipino arts is called a false lead. This is where you look like you are in your normal orthodox stance, but your legs are reversed. Meaning your foot on the jab side is to the rear while your upper body stays fixed with your jab side to the front. The movement of your feet would be like a Thai switch kick.

This is very deceptive and subtle because by switching your left foot to the rear allows more reach for your right cross to hit your attacker without moving. Your attacker will think that you will need to step forward to connect with your right hand…you won't.

Notice:

The the feet are opposite. The left foot is to the rear while the left (jab) hand is in front.

My philosophy on the street fighting.

The title of this book is called "**Slam's Dirty Boxing for the Street**". However, I do not want to ever stand face to face and square off with an opponent in the street. My goal is not to fight. It is to capitalize on winning and walking away with out having to mix it up and possibly get hit or injured. That means that either I am going to deceptively or preemptively strike first. If I can walk away I will. If the aggressor happens to throw the first attack, I will cover crash and do what I need to as fast as I can.

Preemptive Striking- Hitting first.

"He who strikes firstest is the bestest" – Paul Vunak

Preemptive Attacks:

There are no rules for the street and there is nothing fair or unfair when it comes to physicality in a street environment. After-all your life could be at stake. The word Self Defense has been reevaluated and the new coined phrase is "Self-Offense". Meaning to be pro-active, or preemptive which is a different mind-set. Defending by its very nature is losing, being behind the curve and only being able to react instead of act. Action will always beat reaction. This brings me to preemptive attacks.

If you are in an aggressively heated confrontation that you feel is escalating and you can't walk away; your best bet is to strike first. Never giving your confronter the chance to fight. Remember this book is called "dirty" boxing for the street. "***Be decisive, then dynamically explosive***." Meaning once you make the decision to strike, you go all out; don't second-guess or hesitate. When you strike first, you want to strike hard and fast.

Keys to Striking:

- Don't telegraph the strike. Strike from where your hand is...don't wind up before striking
- Dempsey's Drop Step- to generate more power from the body behind the strike.
- Kenpo Principle: Use soft tools to hit hard targets and hard tools to hit soft targets.

Some Preemptive Strikes with Targets:

Head Butt to the Face
Finger Jab to the Eye
Chin Jab
Face Mash
Cupped Hand Blow to the Jaw or the Ear

Web Hand to the Throat
Kick to the Groin
Diagonal Punch to the Groin
Slap to the Groin

Deception and Surprise (Soft Skills)

Aggressive Preemptive tactics for an aggressor that is in a boxing stance ready to fight. Options for sneaky and deceptive Entries to get off the first punch:
You are in your **"I don't want to fight you"** fence position, hands open.

Note: ***The use of deception and body demeanor is a key component to pull this off. Use the element of surprise. It can be a great equalizer!***
A good time to strike is when he is talking, or you are talking. Talking non-sense will throw an aggressor off their game. By saying something totally out of the blue, that is not related to the situation, something out of context that will throw him off. Usually, it is a question that he must think about. Such as "*Hey man, do you know what the weather is going to be tomorrow?*" "*Did you hear about the new restaurant opening?*"

Do one of these as you are asking the question, or he is trying to say something in response to it.

Option 1:
Vault off your rear leg through "no mans' land" with forward motion and double monkey paw grip his wrists down as you throw a right horizontal elbow across his jaw.

Option 2:
Double slap his fists which will startle him and throw him off momentarily for you to land a preemptive hook to his jaw.

Option 3:
Step offline with you left foot and monkey paw the inside of his left forearm down as you throw a right hook to his jaw.

Examples of preemptive sequences on the following pages.

Preemptive Sequences

1 Fence Position

TIP:
Notice that I am monitoring the aggressor's right arm as I am vaulting.

2 Push off rear foot and vault across "No Mans' Land"

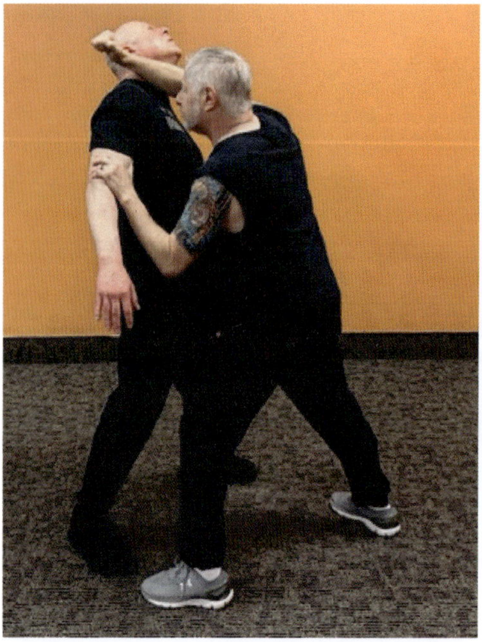

3 Into hacking the side of the aggressor's neck with the outer blade of the forearm and creating a frame to control him. The hack is a good stun strike and it also knocks him off balance.

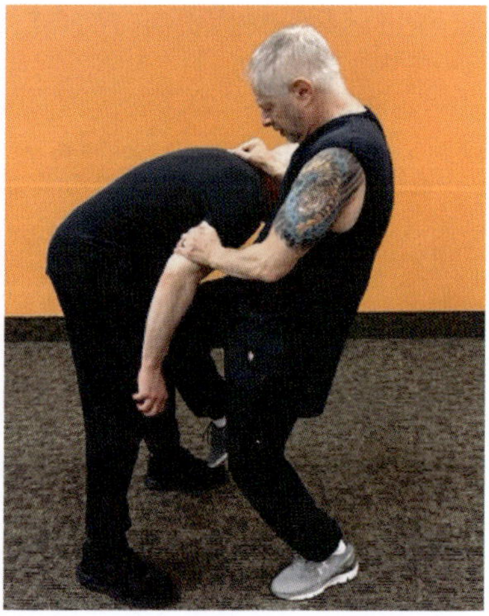

4 Hook behind his neck and pull him down into a knee to the groin.

TIP:
Since you are vaulting at the opponent, the hack should have the full weight of your body's forward momentum.

Preemptive Sequence 2

4-Strike Preemptive Attack

I got this from Kelly McCann. When done correctly it is a super fast 4 strike preemptive attack that will leave your aggressor on the ground wondering what happened or knocked out.

1 Fence/Stand Off

2 Quickly reach with both arms past the aggressor. Hands open.

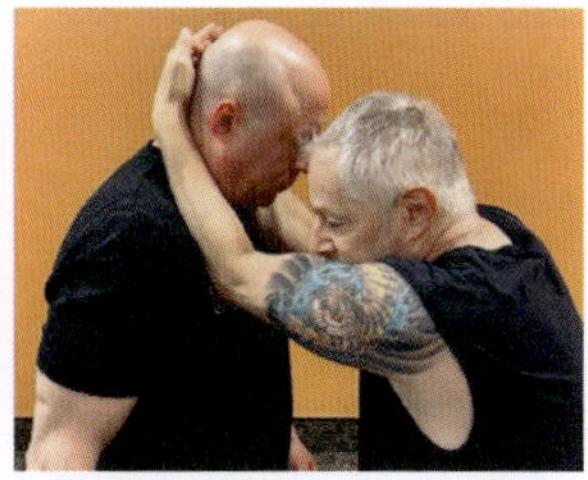

3 Double slap the base of the skull.

4 Continue to pull him into a head butt.

5 Slam him into a shoulder smash.

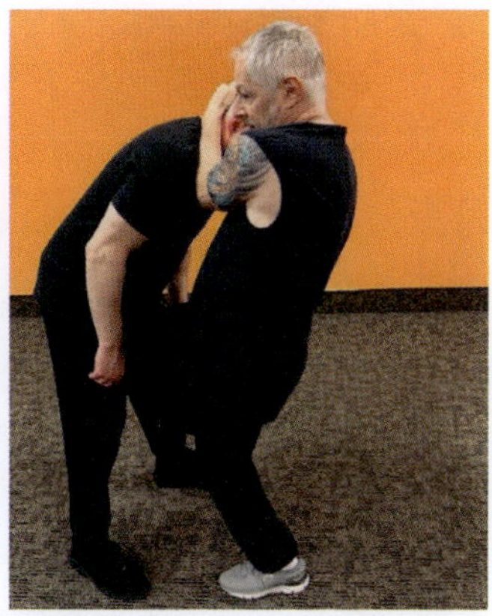

6 While kneeing him in the groin.

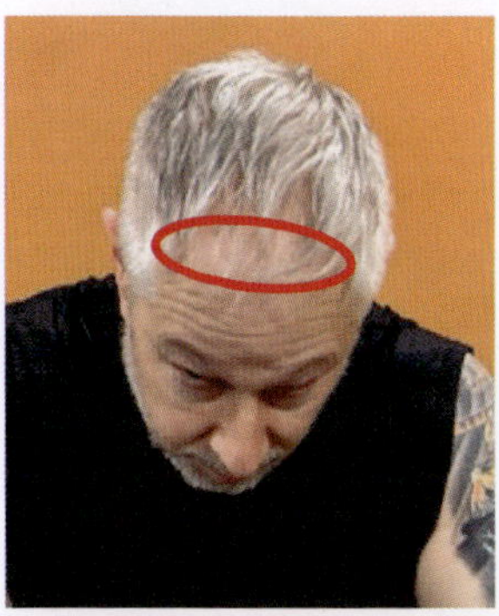

Head Butts

The correct point of contact for a head butt is the crown of the head, around the hair line area. Use that area to smash into the aggressor's nose, not his head. The key is to use your whole body. Do not whip your neck or you will hurt yourself.

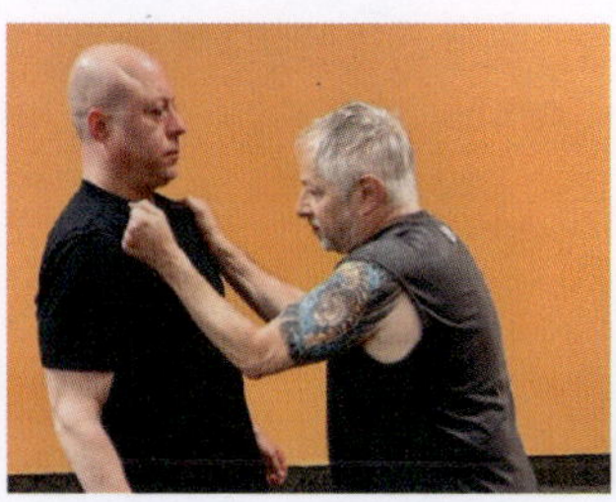

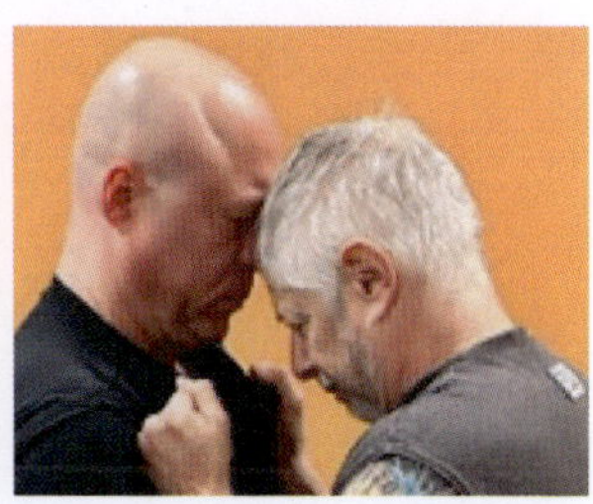

Preemptive Sequence 3

Swivel Punch

This is another preemptive attack that is done from the side. Your hand is out keeping the aggressor at bay from coming into your space. It is also used as a guide for your punch. The name comes from swiveling your hips and generating a great deal of power from your torso. As I turn to face my opponent my left foot steps to the outside setting my hips up for a powerful vertical punch to his solar plexus. Use it in conjunction with being deceptive and pretending to walk away. then explode the punch in. I have seen Lee Morrison demonstrate this punch. He told a story of being in an elevator where someone was blowing smoke in his face after he asked them not to. As you can imagine the guy was left on the elevator floor gasping for breath.

Preemptive Sequence 4
Bowling For Dollars

The name is because the downward strike to the groin is the same as swinging a bowling ball. First I pull the aggressor into a chin jab, and from that strike I use a wind-up swinging motion to slap the groin. This uses the high/low principal.

1 I quickly hook the aggressor's arm and pull him....

2 Into a chin jab.

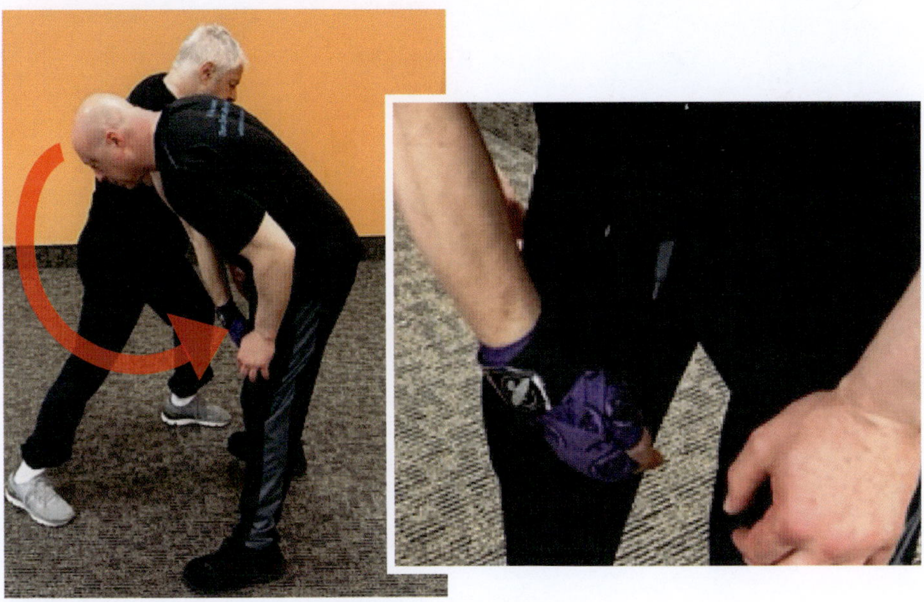

3 Which I then swing clockwise and downward to slap his groin in a bowling motion.

Preemptive Sequence 5

Hook Arm Into Abdomen/Groin Punch

The arm hook should be done very fast and used with deception. It is similar to the arm drag. The idea is to pull the aggressor into the groin punch with the car crash effect. This is another Kelly McCann sequence. There are other finishes that can be done after the groin punch than what is shown.

1 Fence Position

2 Hook Triceps

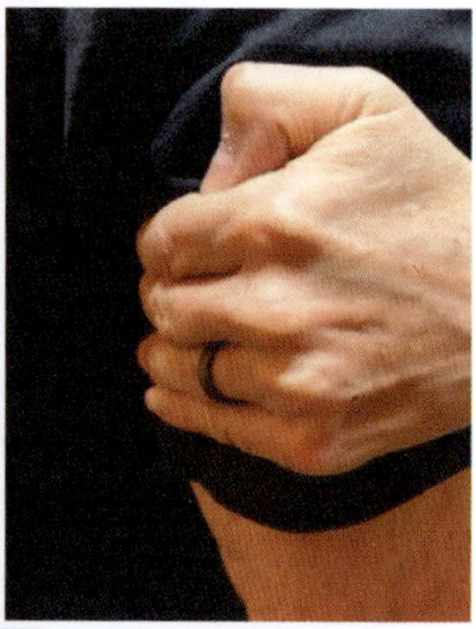

Close up of hook or monkey paw grip

3 Pull the arm towards you as you punch the groin area.

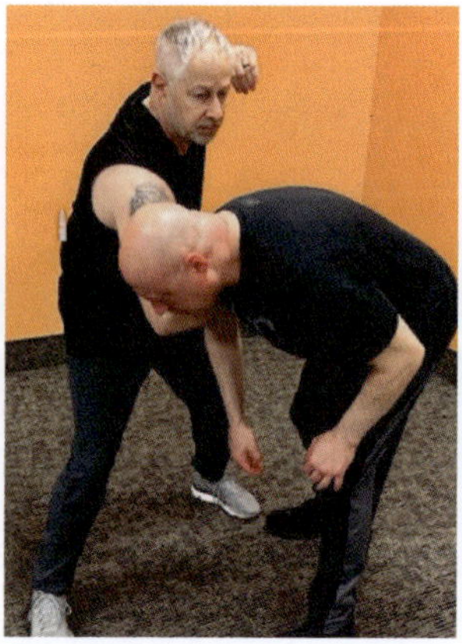

4 I quickly switch hands and continue to hook the arm with my right hand.

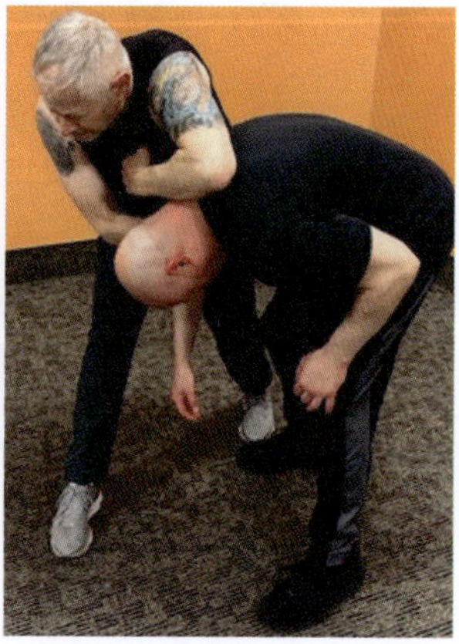

5 I turn and drop weight while elbowing downward to the base of his skull.

TIP:
The punch to the abdomen/groin area should be thrown on a downward angle to cause the most damage.

Note:
This is not a good sequence to use if the aggressor is moving his arm, or his arms are up because it will be very difficult to hook.

Preemptive Against Aggressive Stances

1 The aggressor has brought his hands up into a boxing stance showing his intentions.

2 I quickly step into No Mans' Land as I slap his fists downward.

3 What makes this work is deception, surprise and speed.

TIP:
Part of your training should be working on "**Soft Skills**". Acting, body language, verbal de-escalation and deceptiveness. When his fists come up, act like you don't want to fight, or are not going to. Then simultaneously step in and slap his fists down and throw the elbow.

4 I continue going forward (Dempsey drop step) with a horizontal elbow to the chin.

HELPFUL TECHNIQUE
Key to Striking Harder:

Jack (Dempsey Drop Step) is a step forward like a falling motion using the body's weight behind the strike. This will give you a much more powerful strike instead of just using the limb.

Preemptive Against Aggressive Stance 2

I can't emphasis the use of deception enough in order to make these preemptive attacks work. This is a slight variation of the previous preemptive sequence. Here the aggressor is showing that he wants to fight. My reaction is my hands are up and open (non-combative). ***I don't want to fight!***
As I am saying this I take my two hands and violently slap his fists. Hopefully, this will shock him enough for me to land a horizontal elbow, or a hook to his jaw. Some Western boxers do this before the match starts when shaking gloves for intimidation and shock value purposes.

Preemptive Against Aggressive Stance 3

This move is a quick step off line away from the strong arm. As I am stepping my left hand hooks the inside of his left forearm and pulls it down simultaneously, opening him up for a right hook to the jaw, or temple.

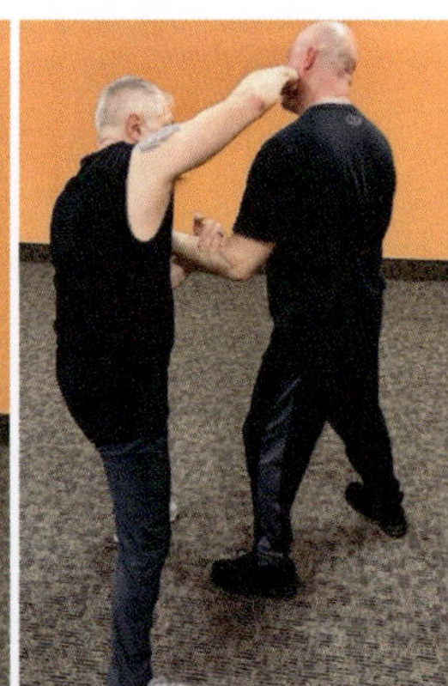

Hook the inside of his left forearm and pull it down!

Preemptive Against Aggressive Stance 4

This move is a similar move to the previous. One might be more comfortable for you than the other. I take a quick step off line away from the strong arm. As I am stepping my left hand hooks the outside of his left forearm and pulls it down simultaneously, opening him up for a right cross to the jaw, or temple. This can also be a left hammer fist to the aggressor's forearm (destruction) instead of hooking it, and a right inward hammer fist to the head instead of a punch.

Hook the outside of his left forearm and pull it down!

> **Note:**
> Stepping off line for this move requires a larger step to clear the outside of his arm. It also gives you more room to fully twist your hips and load up for a stronger punch.

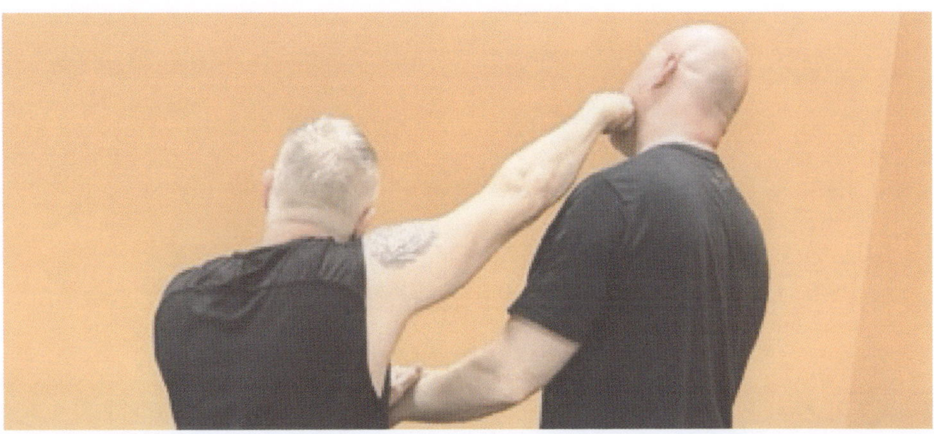

Aggressively Animated

Preemptive Against Aggressive Pointing and Pushing

This move would work for a push as well as a punch. Here the aggressor is upping the scale of his physical aggression by pointing at me. You do not want to let someone start shoving their fingers in your face. Once they are that close it is easy for them to poke you in the eye. Step off the line, and depending which arm is doing the pointing use your mirrored hand and slap it down and across as you vault in with a chin jab. You should be on the outside of the aggressor, perpendicular to him. If he is pushing with two hands, pick an arm and do this same sequence. It does not matter he is using one or two hands. Your goal is to get to the outside of one and hit.

1 Fence Position

2 Step off the line and slap his arm down and across with your mirrored hand.

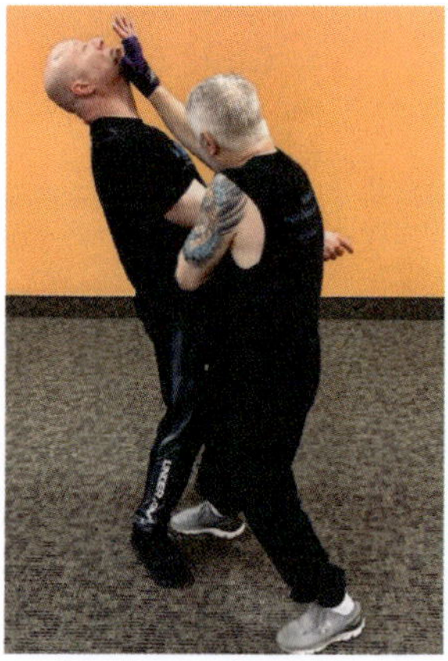

3 Vault forward and chin jab with the opposite hand, staying on the outside of his arm

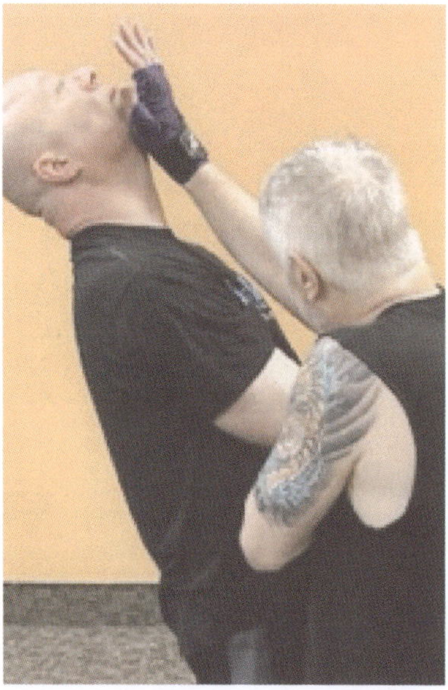

Note:

Your slapping arm should be under your chin jabbing arm. Also, my slapping hand is pushing and maintaining control of his pointing arm the whole time.

Preemptive Against Aggressive Slapping Your Hands Down

This time your aggressor is doing the slapping. I call this the three stooges move. Funny, not funny! I have seen Lee Morrison do this. The aggressor is building up his scale of violence and is now getting physical by slapping your hands down. When he slaps your dominant hand be relaxed and let the force of the momentum swing back up hitting the aggressor's ear with a cupped hand blow. The harder he hits your hand, the faster and harder he is going to be hit.

1 Fence Position

2 The aggressor is really getting animated and is starting to slap your fence down.

3 Relax your dominant hand and let the force of the momentum of his slap accelerate a cupped blow to his ear.

4 Since my hand is already on the side of his head, I throw a left elbow, sandwiching his head. When you hold one side of the head and hit the other side it causes more damage since the head can't move away from the strike.

Cover and Crash

Blocking like traditional martial arts takes too long and requires practice, timing and skill. It is easy to miss and wind up eating the punch. Covering like boxers do is a more solid way to handle punches speeding at you.

Supported Elbow Frame Cover

This cover works best for a rounded punch, such as a haymaker or a hook. Your left arm is bent with your hand cupping over the ear and the back of the neck. The elbow is positioned in front of your nose and facing the attacker, which means your left eye is covered as well. You will be seeing with your right eye. Your right arm goes across your face like a face guard on the football helmet, and your right hand is cupping (bracing) your inner forearm above the elbow. This supported frame with crashing forward will give you the best results. Sometimes the punch is too fast or your timing is off. That is ok as long as you are covered. In the real world you will not always be able to crash in.

Supported Elbow Frame Cover

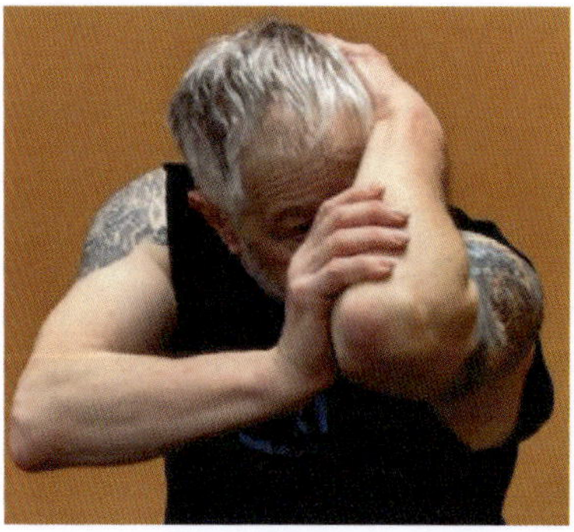

Front View

Side View

This cover came from Joe Simonet.

How to Cover and Crash with a Spearing Elbow

Note: This is all done simultaneously: From the fence index position, cover with the point of your elbow facing your aggressor, bend at the knees and body slightly forward to lower your body (center of gravity), chin is tucked down and teeth are clenched, push off your rear foot and vault your body forward with the point of your elbow impaling your attacker in the upper pectoral muscle or center mass. A common mistake is to push upward instead of forward going through your opponent.

The natural reaction when an aggressor throws a big, rounded punch at you is to step back or lean away, but that does not get you out of the path. It puts you into the hardest hitting point of the swing, toward the end. On a rounded punch you should train yourself to **step into or behind the arch of the swing**. This is an unnatural reaction to go forward, but it is the safest. The actual punch will go past your head if you do this. The closer you are the weaker the punch will be, if it even hits you. Assuming you have some distance, you will be able notice the wind-up motion for the haymaker you can time it and crash in with a ram's horn cover before it gets to the full curve of the arch and knock your aggressor off balance.

Spearing Elbow

This my favorite way to quickly crash through No Man's Land because you are in a covered position. The impact caused by the point of elbow combined with the full weight of your body behind it will not only shock and overwhelm your aggressor, but possibly knock the wind out of him. This can be just a single elbow or a supported one. The spearing elbow is a multi-purpose tool, that can be used as a preemptive strike, or can be used against someone throwing a haymaker at you.

Defense Against a Haymaker
Crashing with the Supported Elbow Frame Cover

1 Fence Position

2 Recognizing the swinging punch as I start to cover for it.

3 Crashing into the arch of the swinging punch with a supported elbow frame.

Notice
Because I crashed into the swinging arch the punch is way behind me.

TIP:
Your goal and your mind-set is to go through him and take his space, as well as impale him with the point of your elbow.

Using the Spearing Elbow Preemptively

From fence stance lower your base and push off with your rear foot,vaulting straight into your aggressor with the point of your elbow impaling him.

TIP:
Lower your center of gravity and when you push off your rear foot make sure that your body is going straight ahead and not upward. Otherwise you will loose the power from your body's weight when crashing.

I had been doing this move for a long time with the Supported Elbow Frame, but the first time that I heard it called "Spearing Elbow" was from Kelly McCann. Lee Morrison calls it a spike elbow. Whatever you decide to call it, it's a move that should be in your fighting tool box.

Covering

Here are some different covers that I have picked up. some of them overlap by doing the same thing. Try them with someone actually swinging punches at you to decide which cover(s) you like best.

Single Cover

The single cove is used of a hook.

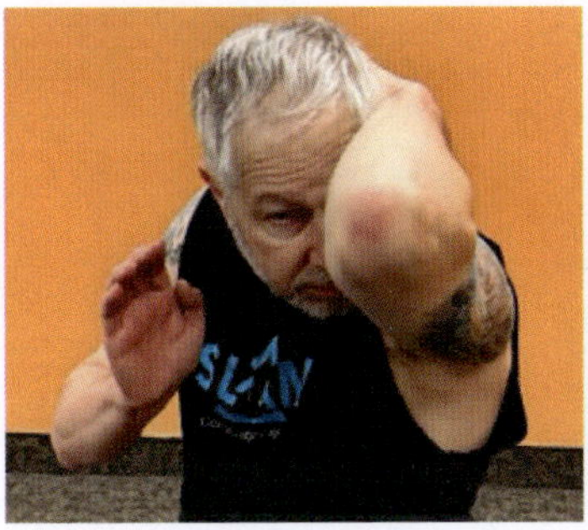

Front View

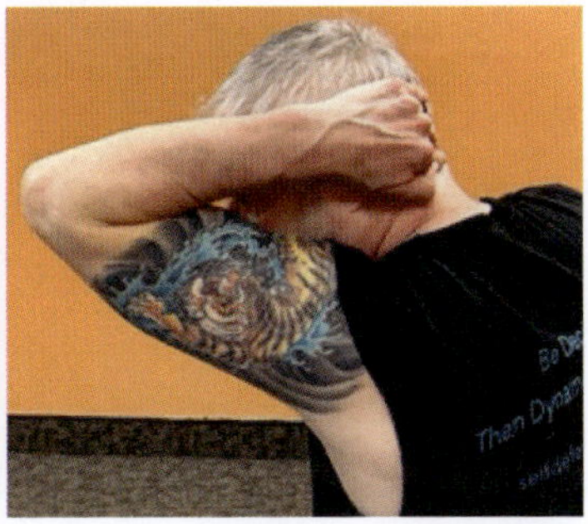

Side View

Ram's Horn

The ram's horn cover can be used in a variety of ways, and against a variety of attacks. To do it correctly the palms of your hands have to be in contact with the top of your skull. I usually use a ram's horn to cover my face if my attacker is throwing straight punches at me. **Note:** You should be able to see through the slit between your arms when covered. Crash in and nullify the punches by closing the distance, cramping the attacker's arms. Usually, my counter is a technique called whirling leaves from Kenpo (to be shown later) which smothers his fists down and gives me an opening for a back knuckle or the blade of my forearm in his face.

Front View

Another use for the ram's horn is crashing into a wide haymaker, or an attacker that is swinging a club. I time the haymaker before the arch I start to crash with my cover into the attacker's biceps.

Front View

Full Cover

The full cover is used to protect the head from a barrage or combination of aggressive hard straight and rounded strikes. It it used when you are not expecting some one to start wailing on you.

Crazy Monkey Defense

Crazy Monkey is a unique defense for a barrage of punches that are coming at you in different directions. Your palms go on top of your head as your elbows constantly move around and cover your head from the punches. A key part is that your palms never loose contact with your head. And yes, if you have hair it will mess it up, but it is better than getting a nose job!

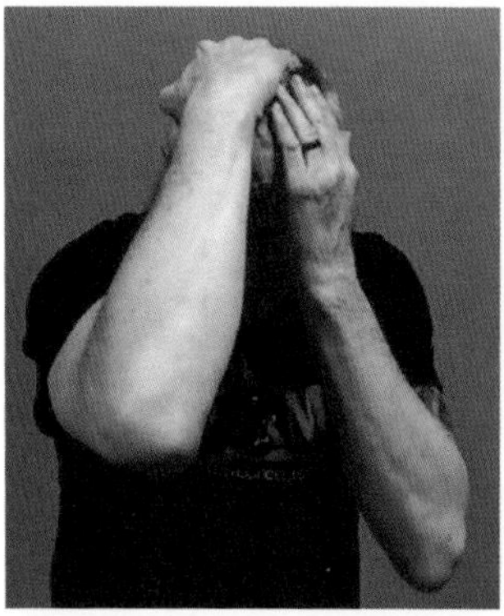

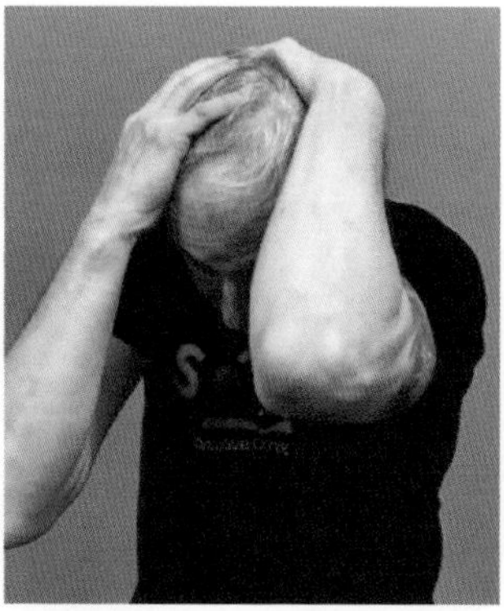

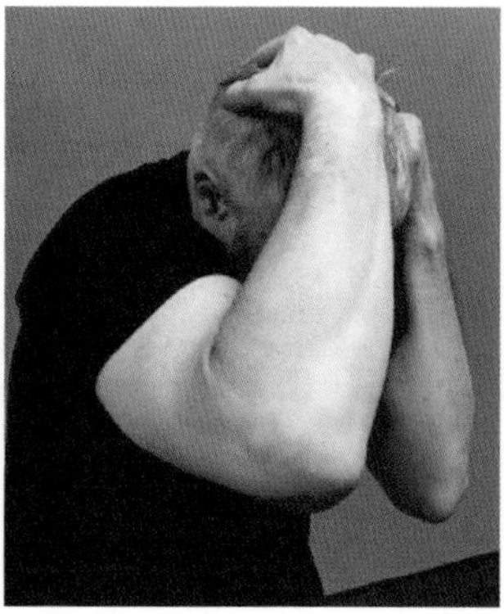

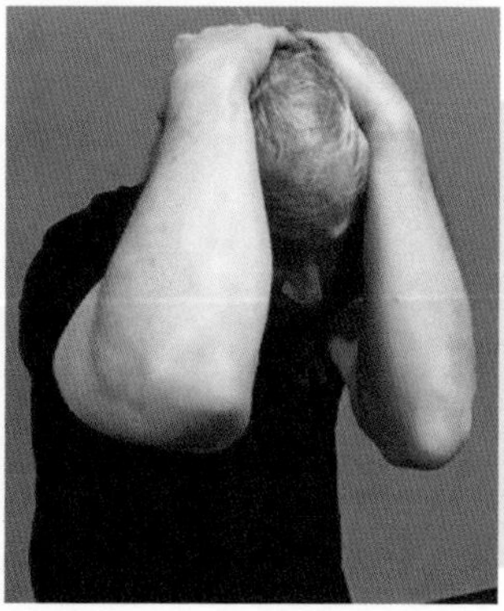

TIP:
Like with all the rest of the covers keep your chin down and teeth clinched. Your eyes should look under your brow at your attacker.

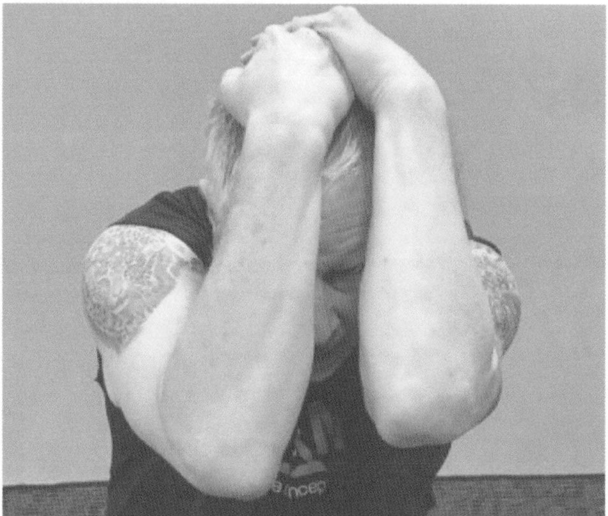

Rams Cover Sequence Against a Haymaker

1 As the attacker begins his swing I cover with both arms and crash before it makes a full arch.

2 After contact my left hand hooks his wrist as my right elbow clips his biceps with an upward motion.

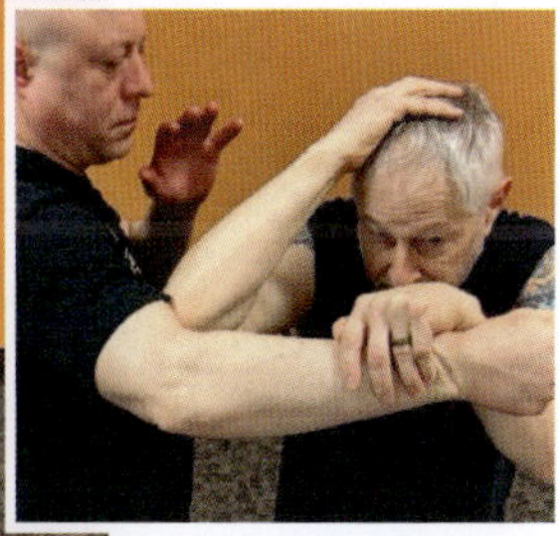

Close up of the biceps clip.
The clip is used as a distraction (tenderizer) to allow me do the next move in the sequence.

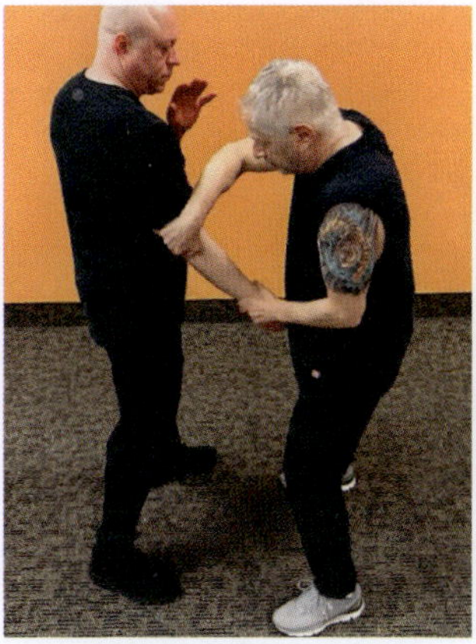

3 I maintain a grip on his wrist as my right hand hooks the back of his triceps.

4 My right hand swings the attacker's arm out of the way while turning him.

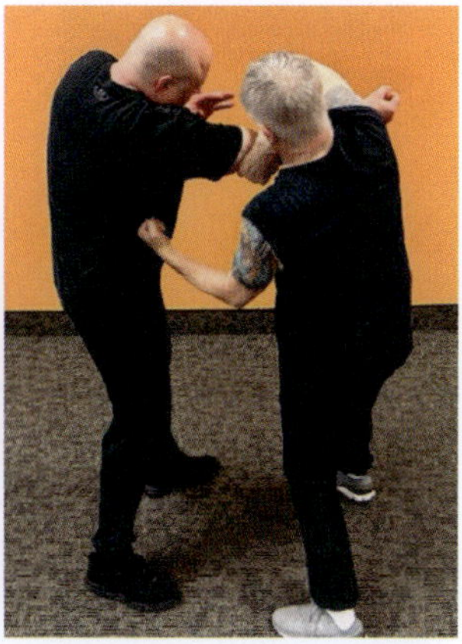

5 And throw shovel hooks to his ribs or kidneys.

Tip:

When crashing the palms of my hands are on the top of my head to absorb the force. If my hands weren't on top of my head during contact, the force would make my own arms bounce back into my face.

Defensive Tools Against Punches

Catch the Jab

Western boxing usually uses a catch for a jab that is coming in. It is quick and you don't have to commit or open yourself up by reaching. It can be used on the street as well, except that you do not have the padding of the boxing gloves to protect your hand from the bare knuckles. So the catch is modified by slightly moving your hand to the side of the punch instead of in front of it .This way the knuckles are not going into your hand.

Note: The catch should only be used on the jab, because as a rule of thumb it is not as powerful as other punches.

Parry the Jab or Cross

Instead of hard blocks such as in traditional martial arts we often use what is called a parry from Western boxing. It is less committal and is a lot quicker. Parries are great to use counters after or simultaneously with. We will get into them in more detail in the entries section. You usually move your head offline as you parry a punch. Your head and your hand should be about 3-6" from each other.

Deflect the Jab or Cross

A deflection is done by stepping offline as the attack comes in. The back of an open hand or arm is used. The movement is like fixing the side of your hair. For instance a punch comes the brushing motion of your hand and arm graze the incoming punch and lets the attack slide past causing the aggressor to go forward and off balance for you to counter. It some instances the attacker punches so hard that he goes past you. Deflections are good to keep your opponent off balance after he throws a hard hit. A deflection can also be used to slow a punch down by meeting the friction of your arm to his. It is possible to slow it down enough to catch the arm.

Intercepting

Intercepting is a Jeet Kune Do (JKD) method of entry. In my opinion it is quite advanced because it takes great timing.

Intercepting the Jab by stepping off line and twisting the hips while diagonally intercepting across (crossing the line) the top of his arm with a finger jab to the eye.

Scoop the Jab

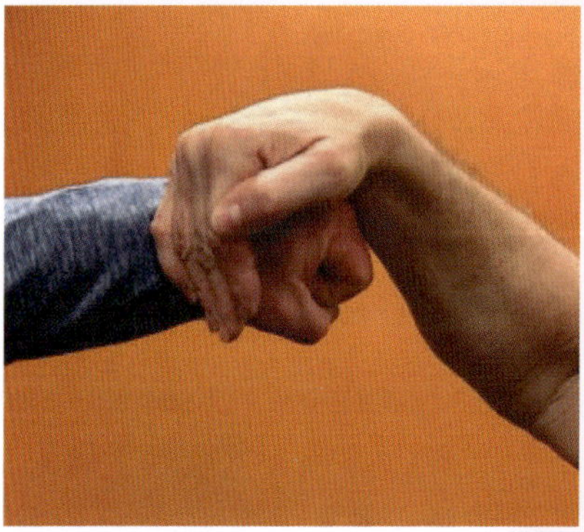

Hand position for scooping the jab.

Half Beat off the scoop to a hook

INFO:
A strike is usually a full beat count. A half beat is used as a fast (ricochet) off the previous strike. It is to break rhythm and add speed.

Footwork

Footwork is an important part of boxing whether in the ring or on the street. As I have said earlier in this book, I am not going to go into full detail of basic boxing footwork. You should already have a decent grasp of the basics. I will show a few unique footwork patterns to compliment the dirty boxing.

Basic Filipino Footwork Drills

The Filipinos use kali sticks to practice footwork patterns. There are many more patterns than what I am about to show here, therefore the patterns can be lined out with masking tape on the floor to follow.

This is the main footwork used to avoid incoming straight punches and is usually used in conjunction with parries or deflections.

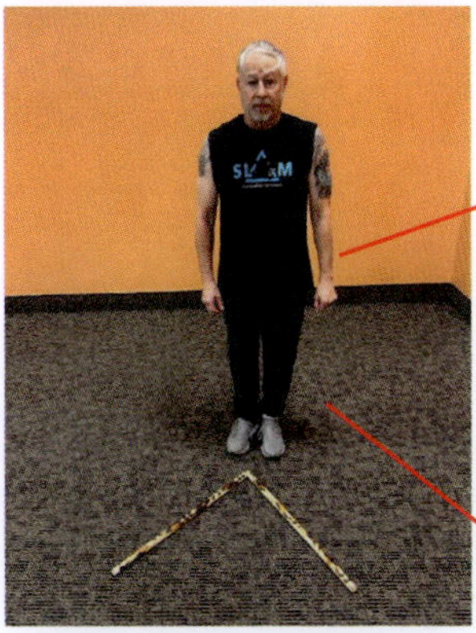

Female Triangle
Notice that the sticks are pointing toward me and the ends are open angled outward.

I step off line at an angle to one side and step back to center. Then I step to the other side and back to center again.

Note:
This is footwork goes forward at the angle to the outside of the incoming punch and puts me toward the side of my opponent. That is where I want to be.

Retreating Footwork

When going back or retreating you should never go straight back. you want to angle off and be offline so you can be allusive to your attacker. Your attacker can go faster forwards than you can go backwards so it doesn't make sense to go straight back when your opponent is aggressively attacking you. Page 82 will give you visual of this using another footwork pattern.

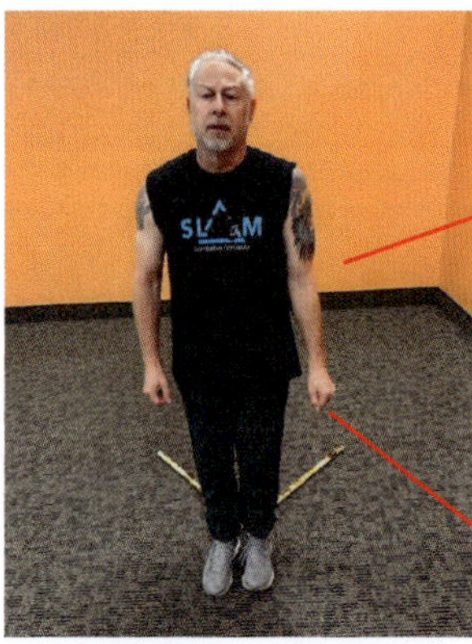

Male Triangle
Notice that the sticks are behind me pointing forward and the ends are angled outward.

I step back off line at an angle to one side and step back to center. Then I step back to the other side and then back to center again.

Lightning Bolt Step (Silat Footwork)

This is a deceptive 1-2 step. **1**. From fighting stance the left foot steps off to the outside of attacker's right rear foot to 10:30. **2**. After it is planted the right foot changes your direction by cutting to 2:00 in between the attacker's legs and taking his space, throwing him off balance. **Note:** This footwork can be done on either side. This footwork works great with a shoulder bump to the ribs or under the arm pit. I learned this step from Burton Richardson's *Silat for the Street*.

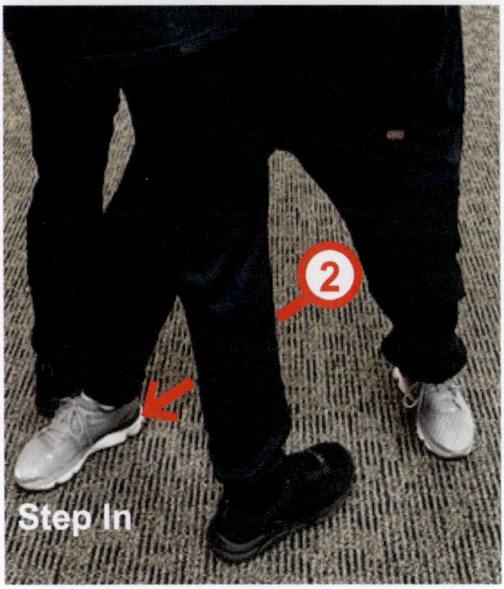

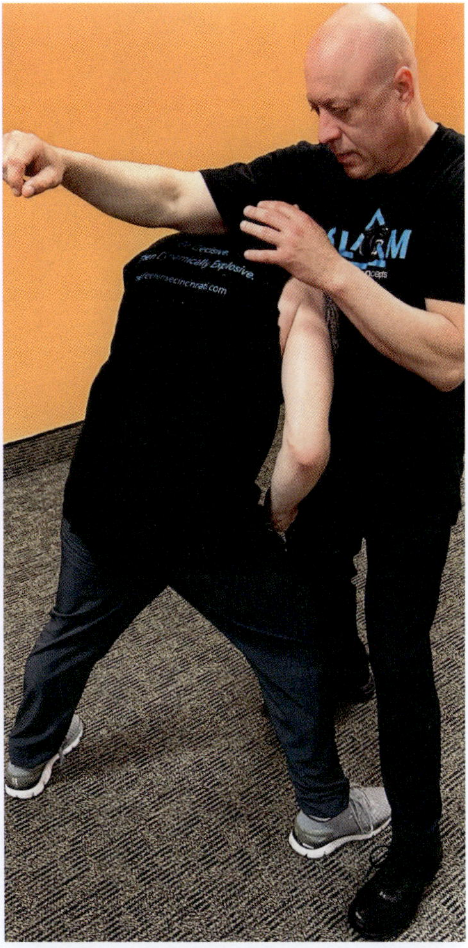

Lightning bolt step with shoulder bump

Opening the Gate Footwork

This is a basic combative foot movement to get out of the way when an aggressive attacker is coming straight at you. You want to make way and get to their side. Quickly step off line and swing your rear foot in an arch until you are facing your aggressor's side in a fighting stance. I believe Kelly McCann coined the phrase "Opening the Gate".

Step Out Off Line

Rear Foot Swings Around

Chinese Kenpo Move Called Dart

This move is against a jab. As the jab shoots toward you step back and cat stance giving you some distance and time to scoop the jab. Immediately spring forward with two fingers to his eye .

TIP:

After the scoop the eye strike shoots right in from the scoop on a half beat.

Make sure that your two fingers are tightly against each other for support in case you miss and hit his skull.

Brush, Grab, Strike on the Inside

This is against a straight right punch. *I am purposefully keeping my left arm down so that what I am doing can be seen*. There is a lot going on here. This sequence must be done fast and explosive because you are on the inside and have to be aware of his left arm. As the punch comes a right hand brushing parry makes contact and is then replaced with the left back hand which brushes down to the attacker's wrist and grabs. The right hand chambers. Pull the arm toward you and step forward between his legs (car crash effect and take his space) as you throw a right hand chop or hack to the side of the neck. Note: If the attacker's left hand comes then your chambered right hand can pick it up or cover.

1 Inside Brush Parry the cross.

2 Follow-up with a left deflection which takes the place of the parry.

3 The left hand slides to the wrist and grabs it

3 Pulling the opponent into a chop or hack to the side of the neck.

Shoulder Roll with a Stop Kick

A shoulder roll with a stop kick. As the person is throwing a punch. Slightly rock back with your shoulder up.

Using Your Head

Using your skull- Not really recommended to stop a punch, but if you can't get your hands up in time, clinch your teeth together, tuck your chin down a let the attacker's fist hit you just above your forehead. It will hurt you a bit, but his knuckles will get the worst of it. The skull is made up of thick hard bone and will break his hand, similar to running it into your elbow.

Tip:
If you have to use your skull make sure that your tongue is out of the way and your teeth are clinched together.

Open Hand Strikes

Bitch Slapping an Aggressor

The use of Slapping is underrated. A cupped slap with good body mechanics behind it can knock someone out just the same as a closed fist. Slapping is better for the street. If you miss with a closed hand punch and happed to hit a hard bone spot you could cause what is called a boxer's fracture (broken knuckles). If you miss with a slap the palm will not break. Also, a keeping your hands open lets you strike faster (looser and more relaxed) than having the tension of a closed fist. Plus, a slap when being witnessed seems less aggressive or violent than a punch. By cupping you hand it will catch air, keep it loose and on contact leave it a little longer than a normal hit for the concussive energy to sink into the target.

A slap to the ear with a cupped hand catches air between the hand and the ear which would force pressure into the ear, popping the ear drum. Pain and loss of equilibrium. Slapping the side of the chin/jaw area with a cupped blow will cause concussive energy to knock out an attacker.

I am not a medical Dr., but I have heard two schools of thought on how knock outs occur: The head whips around fast and the brain which is in fluid hits the sides of the skull causing unconsciousness. The other thought is hitting certain nerves in the neck or head such as the vagus or mental nerve causing unconsciousness.

A hard cupped blow to the back of the skull where it meets the neck (rabbit punch) is not allowed in sport fighting. It is a dangerous strike and can cause an arterial tear and death.
Cupped slap upward to the groin…no explanation needed here.

There are quite a few different variations of open hand strikes, the Chin Jab, face smash, palm heel, claw, cupped hand slaps.

Keys to striking:

Don't telegraph the strike by winding up or moving before. Strike from where your hand is. Use the Dempsey Drop Step for more body power behind the strike.
Kenpo Principle: Use soft tools to hit hard targets and hard tools to hit soft targets.

Chin Jab

The chin jab comes from military combatives and is still a primary tool that is used for self-defense. The chin jab is like a palm heel in the traditional arts. What is so devastating about the chin jab is that it comes under the line of eyesight and is not seen before contact. The accelerated upward motion targets under the chin. (The plan is to knock his head off his neck and shoulders). The attacker winds up having his head whipped back, looking up at the sky.

Face Smash

The face smash is another open hand strike. In traditional martial arts it is usually called a Tiger's Claw. Your fingers are splayed out and rigidly bent. The hitting motion is like throwing a softball. From your hands up position throw from where your hand is (do not wind up). It goes forward and downward slightly smashing into the face. The fingers go to the eyes and the palm of your hand smashes the nose.

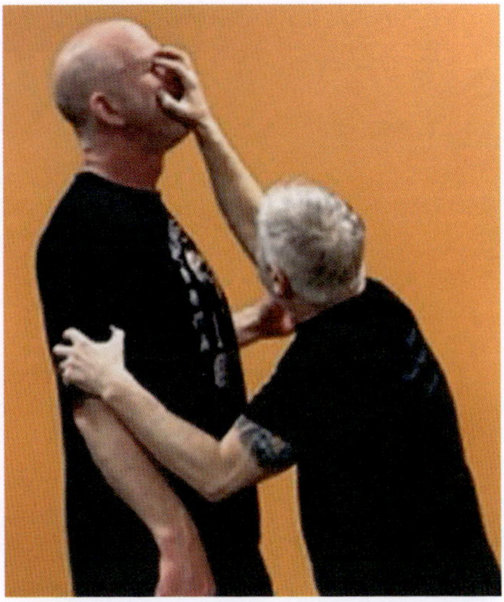

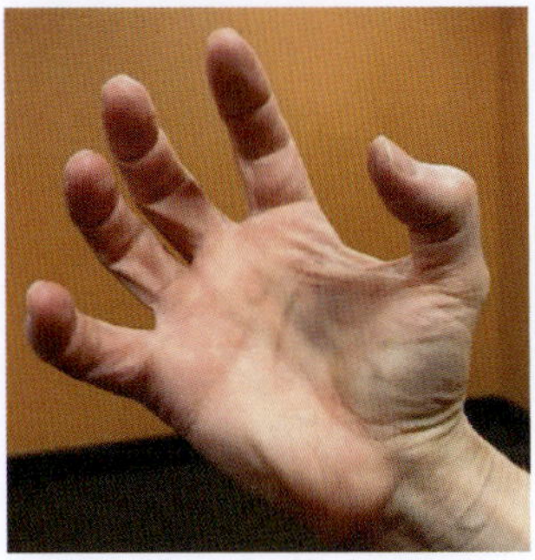

Cupped Ear Slap

The cupped hand slap can be devastating. It will pop the ear drum and mess equilibrium. The hand is actually cupped to gather air in the palm as it makes contact forcing the pressure of the air into the addressor's ear canal creating a seal. The air has nowhere to escape except popping the air canal. It is painful and off balancing.

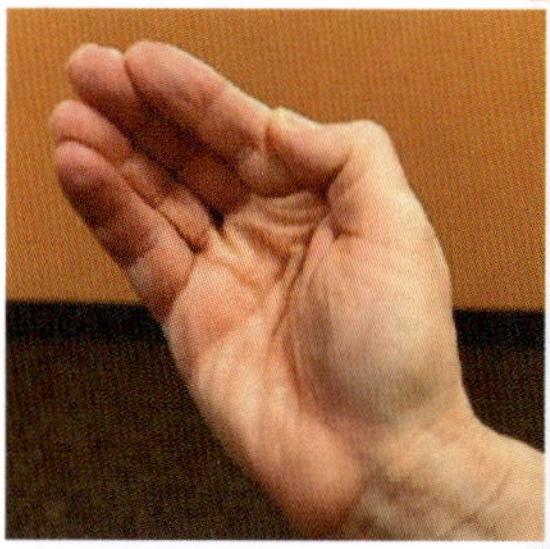

Cupped Hand Position

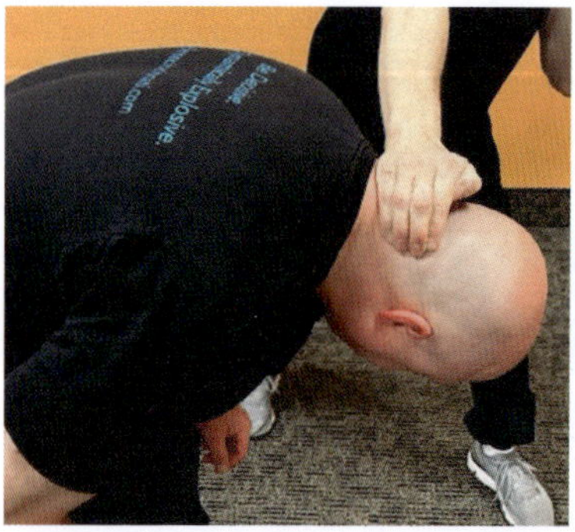

Cupped Slap to the Base of the Skull

The cupped hand slap to the base of the skull could have fatal consequences. In boxing they call it a rabbit punch and is not allowed because there are arteries that could rupture in that area.

TIP:
When slapping try to be relaxed and use a loose wrist and whip the slap in while holding it on the target a second longer than usual.

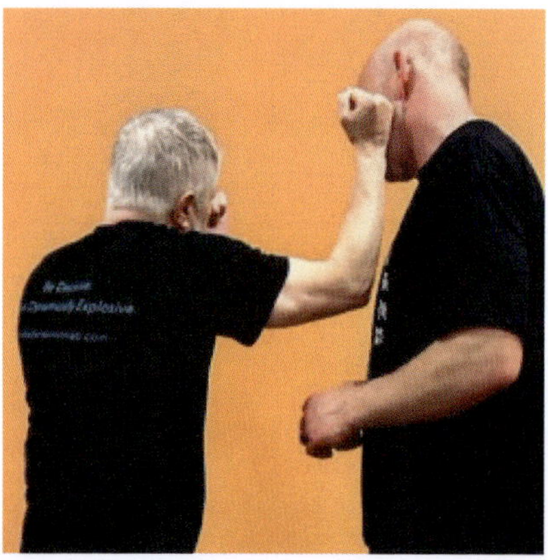

Diagonal Hammer Fist is a closed fist in a diagonal motion for close striking that comes from Filipino knife fighting but works well with empty hands.

Palm Strike

Palm strikes are usually inserted as a half beat to disrupt the opponent's attack, or to push him back and make space for a kick. The strike is meant to send a sudden shock wave to stun the aggressor (Iron Palm Strike) as he is in the progress of throwing a strike. Good timing plays a large part in the success of this strike. I keep the hand (diagonally), fingers facing inward, at an angle instead of upright when I am hitting the face. The reason I do this is because if the palm is vertical when you strike the chest area you will hyper extend your wrist back. I know this from experience. I also use a horizontal palm strike to the aggressor's side of the face, cheek/jawbone area to turn his head away. If he can't see me, he can't fight me. A strong palm shot delivered to the solar plexus can knock the wind out of your opponent.

Tiger's Jaw or Web of the Hand to Throat

The tiger's jaw can we used by shooting the strike to the attacker's throat (larynx) and making contact with the webbing between your thumb and index finger. It can be applied by grabbing the larynx and squeezing it closed. It basically closes off the air way until you let go.

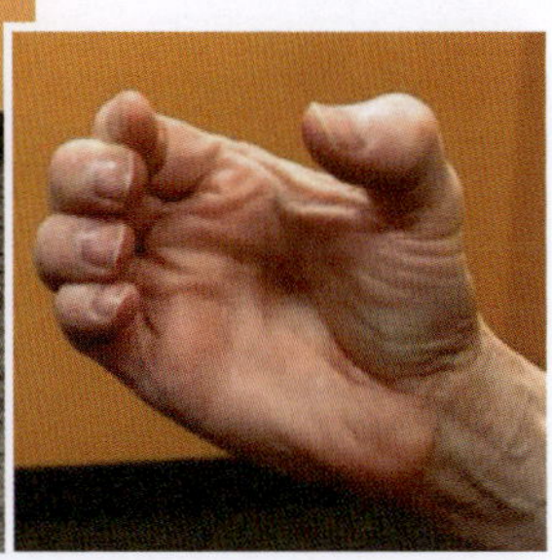

Tiger's Jaw
Hand Position

Chops to the Neck

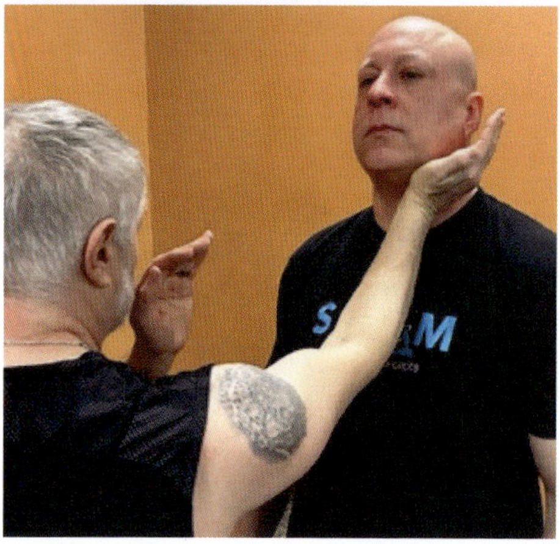

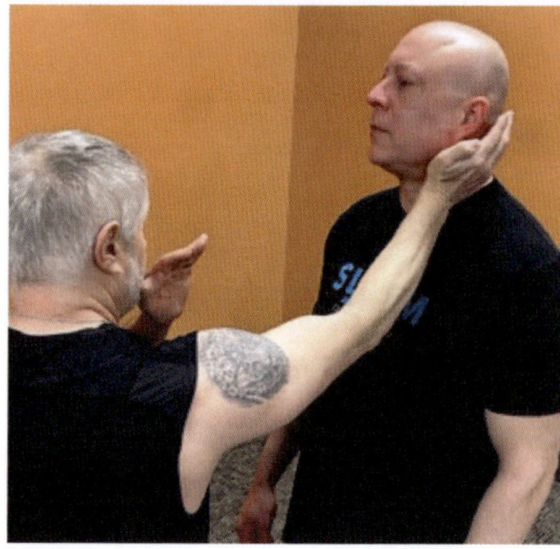

Chop to the Vagus Nerve in the Neck

The palm edge of your hand chops the neck with enough force on the vagus nerve that the aggressor will be knocked out. This target needs lots of practice in order to hit the correct area accurately. The vagus nerve runs down both sides of the neck.

Caution:

If your chop is off and to the left you will hit his trachea (wind pipe) which could be serious.

Chop to the Carotid Artery in the Neck

The carotid artery is more on the side of the neck and on both sides. They are contained within the carotid sheath behind the sternocleidomastoid muscle. With enough force in your strike you can knock someone out. Since it is behind the largest muscle in the neck it is not as easy as the vagus nerve, for a knockout, but it is an easier target to strike.

Tip:

When throwing a chop if you keep the strike on the target longer the energy from the strike will sink in which will more likely cause a knock out than just snapping the strike.

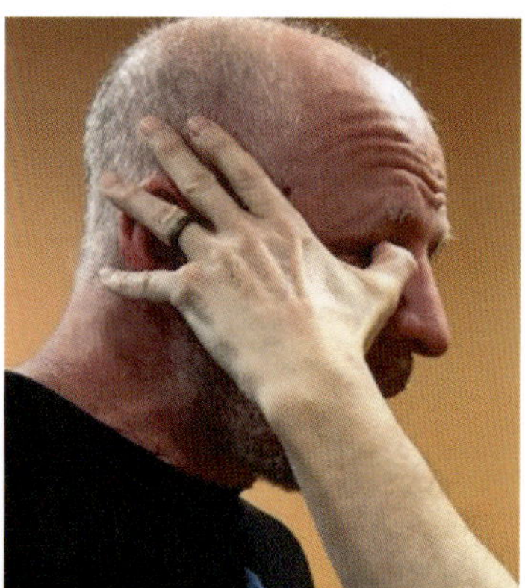

Eye Gouge or Eye Lid Rake

For an eye gouge use your bent thumb push it into the attacker's eye socket. To Rake the eye lid use the finger nail of your thumb and scratch the lid.

Low Line Kicks and Attacks

Kicks are great for the street as long as you keep them low. They can be used as distractions or finishes.

Oblique Kick

This kick is prominent in Jeet Kune DO (JKD). In my opinion it is one of the best self defense kicks that you can throw. It is a low, fast kick. Usually thrown to the shin of your opponent. The kicking motion is similar to kicking a soccer ball. Your inner bottom edge of the foot makes contact with the shin. It is a great set-up kick. Meaning your average aggressor doesn't think of being hit low which makes them react and look down after being kicked because the kick smarts. You also lean slightly away from your attacker when throwing this kick.

Notice:

The slight lean away from my aggressor when kicking creating some distance just in case he throws a punch.

Front Snap Kick to the Groin

This kick is seems to always be available if the person is close enough. Snap the kick upward at the groin using the knee as a hinge. The faster you shoot the kick out and back the less likely it is to be blocked and you to be off balance.

Note:

When kicking always have your hands up to protect yourself.

Front Push Kick

This kick is used to keep someone at bay when they are aggressively coming toward you. The leg is lifted with the knee and then pushed out toward the attacker. It is the same kick you would use to kick a door in.
The primary contact point is the pelvis area (hip bone) to push him back and fold him over. My foot on this kick is to get the hip bone by angling my foot to the right instead of straight up.

TIP:
If you turn and angle the foot you are standing on outward the kick will reach another
6"-12" further.

Round Kick or Round House Kick

The round kick is a martial arts staple. Keep it fast, low and go through the target. A great place to attack with this kick is the inner or outer thigh area.
A well placed kick to the peroneal nerve can put your attacker on the ground.

TRICK:
If you angle the kick downward towards the ground on the outer thigh it causes more pain.

Side Kick

A side kick to the inside or the outside of the knee will cause damage and the attacker will not be able to stand to fight. Not to mention the pain. A lot of people already have some kind of knee problem from sports, or other activities, wrecks etc. You can tell by the way they walk. Those are the kinds of weaknesses that you should look for and exploit in your aggressor.

Knee to Inner Thigh or Knee Knock

The attacker grabs to clinch and refuses to let go. Since the upper body line is closed the lower body line is open. I use a step through knee into his thigh to buckle him off balance and make space.

Notice how his ankle is bent after the knee.

Scoop Kick

The scoop kick goes primarily to the groin. The foot goes under and behind the scrotum and then point the toes upward as you pull out ripping the scrotum.

Front Knee to Groin

The front knee in a very close encounter is the bread and butter of combatives/dirty boxing. To make full contact use the knee pointing forward into the groin instead of upward.

Round or Curved Knee

The round or curved knee is a great close range, low line strike to the attacker's leg or ribs, and can be used in the clinch as a tenderizer or as a set up. These knees are used when the upper line is closed leaving the low line open for these knee attacks.

Round Knee

The round knee is he same movement as a round house kick, except it can be use at very close range (clinch range).

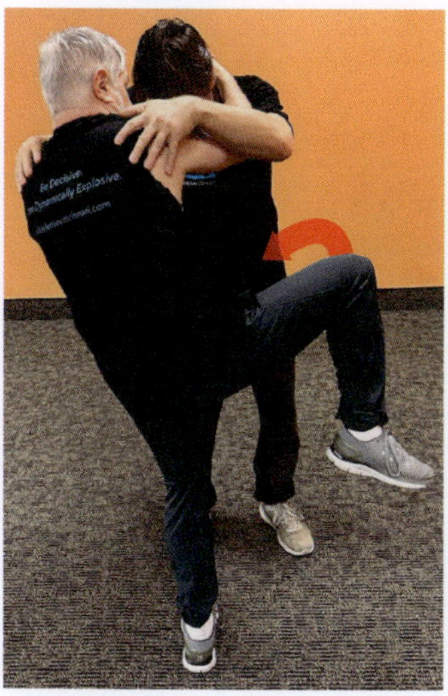

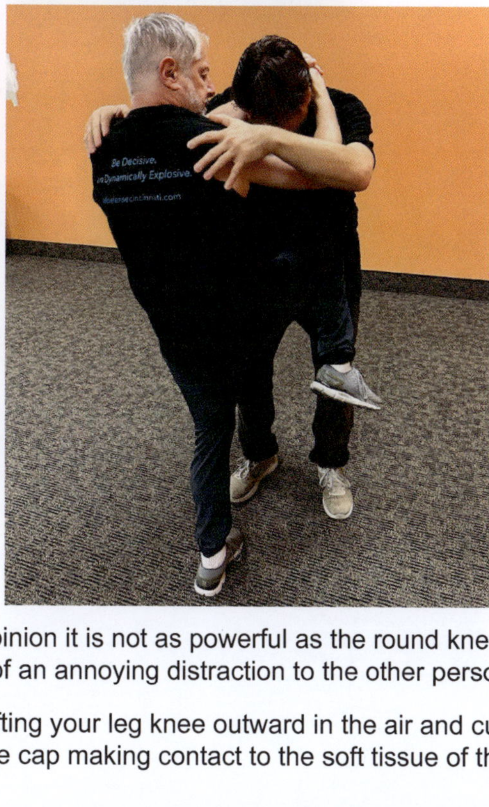

Curved Knee

The curved knee is a good low line strike to the attacker's leg or ribs. In my opinion it is not as powerful as the round knee, but it will cause pain. It is an more of an annoying distraction to the other person.

The curved knee is done by lifting your leg knee outward in the air and curving it inward with the side if the knee cap making contact to the soft tissue of the outer leg or the ribs.

Foot Trap

A foot trap is a great low line, low profile attack. Step on the aggressors foot and push him. If you push him hard and keep your foot weight on top of his, the aggressor will fall over and break his ankle, ending the fight. Here I use it against a cross by deflecting the punch and stepping on the his foot while pushing him at an angle. Notice how it makes him cross his legs and really unbalance his stance.

PREEMPTIVE TIP:
If you are at a stand off you have to be able to step on his foot without looking down at the aggressor's feet. You don't want to show your intentions. This is where your Peripheral vision comes in.

Foot Stomp

If the upper parts of the body are tangled up, branch to the lower parts of the body. The foot stomp is a way to keep your attacker's attention on his foot instead of focusing the fight up top. Another variation to this is using your foot to scrape down his shin and stomp the foot.

Kick Defenses

With the rise of combat sports everyone that is either a fan or watches MMA, tries to throw kicks at the gym heavy bags in hopes to use them. Being able to deflect or shield a kick is important for the street for that reason alone.

Shielding Against a Round Kick

As the round kick comes bring you knee up and towards the kick while push outward. Pushing outwards on his leg will disrupt his balance.

Note:
My arms are up and in some cases if the kick is higher I will touch my elbow to the top of my knee creating a full barrier of my body.

You can also use your front leg to shield the kick.

TIP:
Shielding a hard kick is no fun! Shin bone to shin bone hurts. If you can angle you shin when the kick makes contact it may slide the kick downward instead of flush bone on bone.

Catching the Front Kick

My attacker goes to throw a front kick at me. Whether it is a front push or snap kick I move off the line of its path. I swing my arm in a low blocking motion with my hand hooking and catching the leg, leaving him on off balance on one leg. I then shoot a side kick into the back of the knee cap of his standing leg dropping him.

1

2

3

4

Stopping the Mid-Level to High Round Kick

This is for a mid-level to high kick defense. As the kick is coming I step away from it and into the arch. I forcefully use my the palms of my hands on his thigh to stop the kick in mid-arch and possibly throw him off-balance.

1

2

3

4

Limb Destructions

Limb destructions are a very violent and painful way to make your attacker wish that they never attacked you.

The Mind-set is fierceness.
"Whatever is thrown at me I will destroy!"

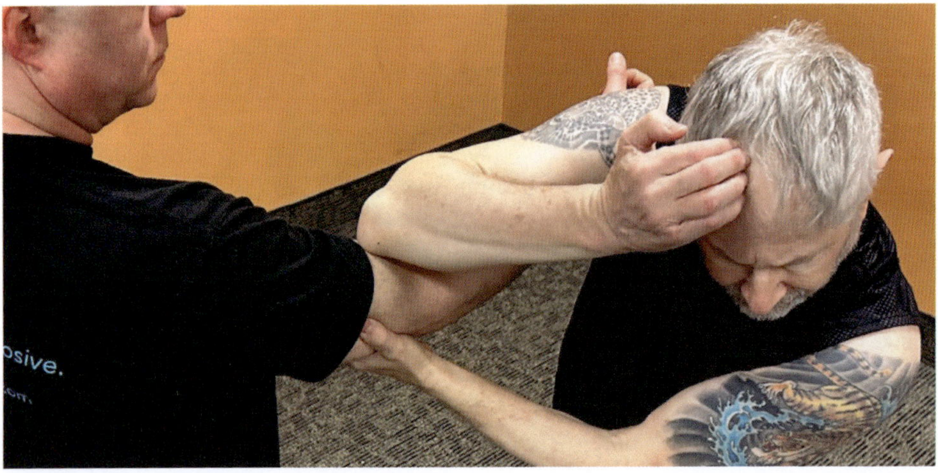

Hammer Fist Destruction

Make a tight solid vertical fist and hit with the bottom part of it like a hammer. As soon as something (punch or kick) comes at you smash it! Caveman like. It is very brutal on the forearms and hands. There are a lot of nerves on the top of the forearm, when hit causes great pain. A good shot to the forearms and your attacker will be hesitant to stick that arm out again.

Hammer Fist Destruction

As the Jab comes, step off line and twist the hips while using a hammer fist to smash down on either his forearm or the top of his fist.

Gunting

Gunting is a Filipino term that means scissors or scissoring. It comes from fighting with blades and is adapted to the empty hands. It is a motion in which you parry or deflect a punch with one hand and hit a vulnerable part of a limb with the other. The hand position can hit with the first set of knuckles, the second set of knuckles, or we can use what is known as an eagle's beak in Kenpo.

Gunts like elbows can hit vertically or horizontally. As you will see, you can also hit on the inside of the arm or the outside. Some of what I call gunts in this book are not "scissoring" motions, but strikes to various areas of the limbs. We will start our way at the bottom with the hands and work our way up the arms.

Gunts to the Wrist and Hands

This is a gunt to the underside of the wrist. As the opponent punches you quickly flick your fist out and upward to hit under the wrist. There are nerves under the wrist. You can also take your second set of knuckles and hit to the top of the hand. These are not "end all" strikes, but they are an annoyance and can lead to follow-up openings.

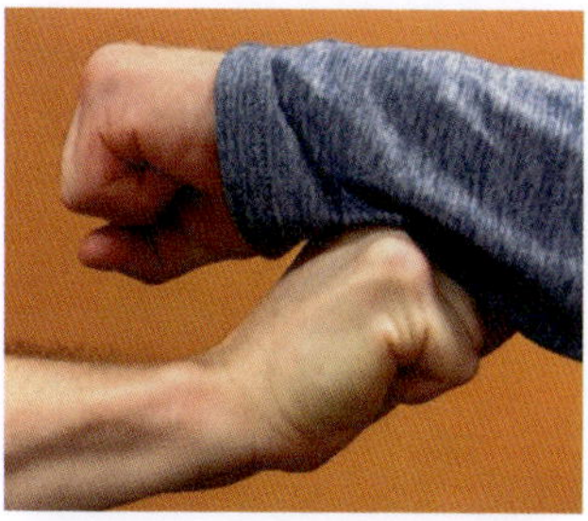

Close-up of the top of the fist hitting under the wrist.

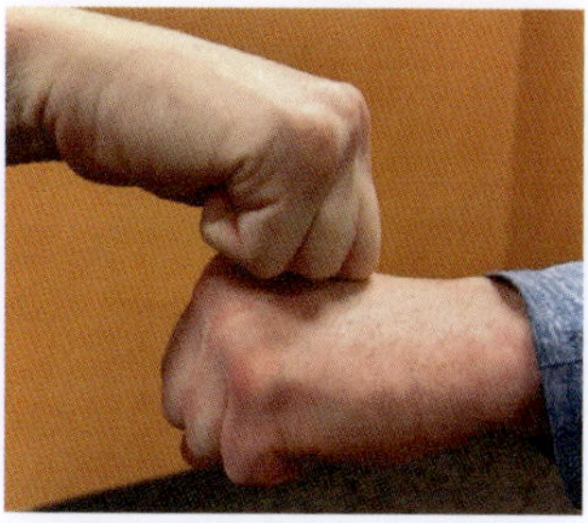

Close-up of the second set of knuckles hitting down on top of the hand.

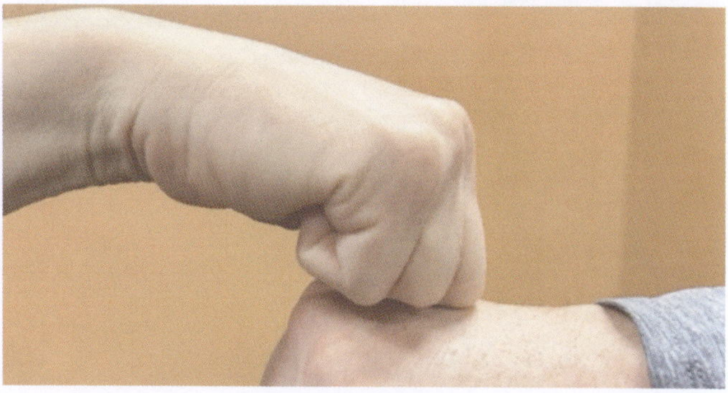

Gunts to the Biceps

This is a **inside horizontal gunt** to the biceps. Notice that I parry the punch from hitting my face first. Then I strike the biceps with what is basically a back knuckle. The top set of knuckles strike into the biceps.

Gunts to the Triceps

This is a **outside horizontal gunt** to the triceps. This is done in the same manner as the inside gunt to the biceps with the back knuckles hitting the triceps.

This is a **outside vertical Gunt**

Note:
If you hit the correct spot (the funny bone) he will get that hot, shocking sensation as when you bang your elbow on something. It is easier to hit that area with a vertical gunt.

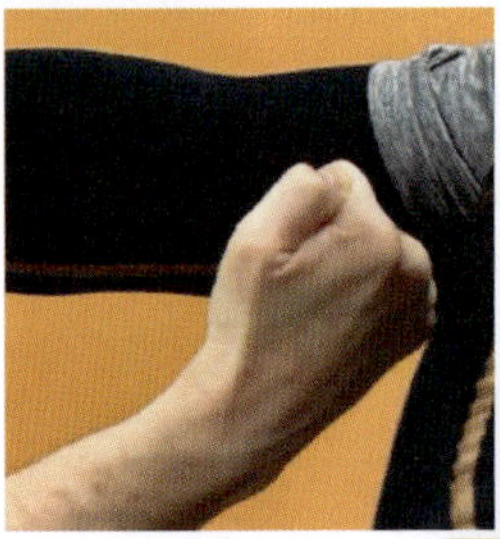

This is called a **Crossada**. This is the actual scissor motion that the meaning gunt comes from. As the punch is thrown you step off line and parry. At the same time you are going to hit through the biceps. The second set of knuckles are used.

Upper Cut to the Biceps

As the attacker throws the cross step offline to 11:00 and parry with the left hand. Use the right to throw an upper cut to the attacker's inner biceps/ triceps area

Cover Elbow Flair to the Biceps

This is a dirty, easy and very effectively painful insert into a cover. As you cover the elbow flairs outward so that the point lands right into the attacker's biceps when he throws his haymaker. The harder he throws his punch the more pain he will be in. The attacker will not want to throw that arm again. Give it a try. Even the lightest swing into the elbow point will hurt.

This is one that sometimes students accidentally do to each other in training. You can't take more than a few of these before your arm is dead.

Vertical Punch to the Biceps

As the attacker throws a hook, cover and throw a vertical punch at his biceps.

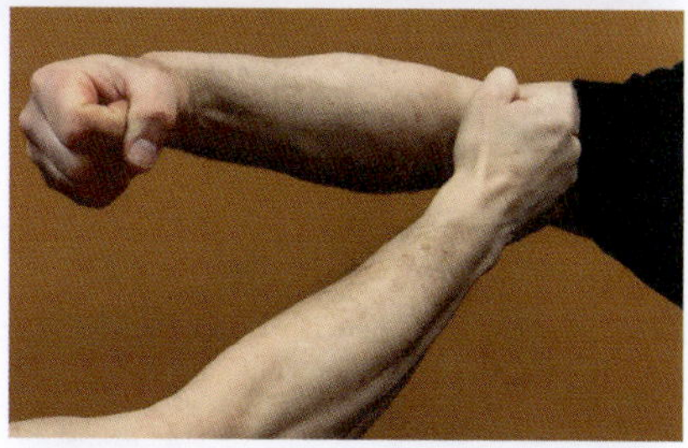

Close up of a vertical punch to the biceps

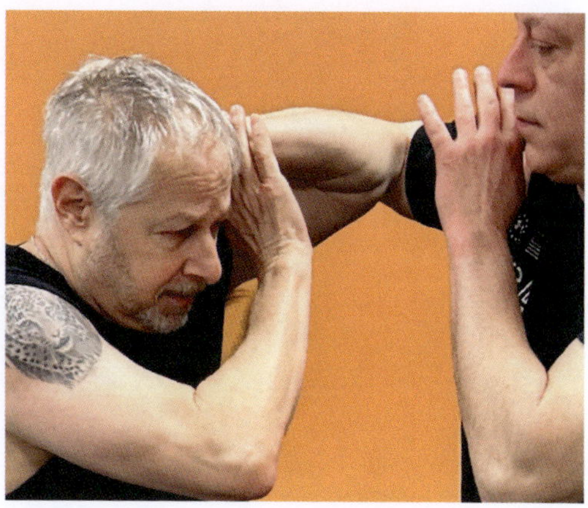

Vertical Elbow

If I am throwing a **vertical elbow**, I usually like to mirror my attacker's punch (same side). If he is throwing his left jab at me, I am smashing it with my right **vertical elbow**. One reason for the same side vertical elbow is because it is fast and can meet the speed of the jab. I usually throw the **horizontal elbow** from the opposite side of the attacker's punch. The attacker throws his right cross, I am smashing it across with a right **horizontal elbow**.

Elbow Destruction

Keep your arms slightly higher then the boxing stance. Align your elbows higher and closer to the line of where the punch will be going. Have your attacker run his fist right into the point of your elbow.

TIP:
Feeding into the Elbow

I will also use my other hand to help feed or steer his fist into my elbow. In this case the left hand will feed into the right vertical elbow.

Horizontal Elbow

Both arms are held high, and as the cross comes, I feed the fist and twist my hips as the point of the right horizontal elbow sandwiches the attacker's fist.

To make this destruction powerful, make sure that you twist with your hips while throwing the elbow. The area of contact when throwing an elbow should be the hard pointed end, not the forearm. The sharp bone end of an elbow can cut a person when it makes contact.

1 Fence Position

2 Arms and hands go up high to begin to align the elbows with the cross line of fire.

TIP:
To throw a good horizontal elbow to where the point is the area that hits the target, the hand and wrist flex downward as you are throwing the elbow. A training method is to have the thumb rotating on the chest when throwing the elbow. This will help to keep the hand and wrist flexed so you will strike with the hard point of the elbow. It also helps to keep the elbow tight to the body.

3 The left hand feeds the incoming fist as the hips fully twist with the right horizontal elbow smashing into his right fist.

Elbow Destructions

Elbows are devastating weapons when wielded correctly. The elbows are used to destroy your attacker's fists. Whether the elbow is horizontal or vertical you want to make your attacker's fist run into the hard pointed part. Break his knuckles with your elbow. This causes what is known as a **boxer's fracture**. Elbows can also be used on the attacker's forearm, biceps, or triceps area. It's a very painful experience.

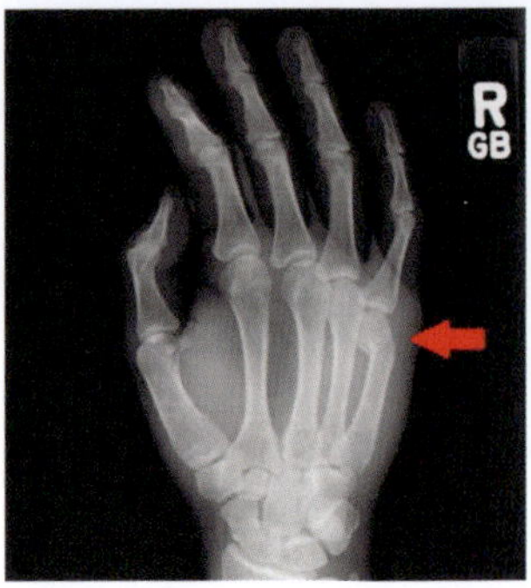

X-ray of Boxer's Fracture

Forearm Destructions Against Fighting Stance or Covers

If your aggressor has shelled up with a tight cover you can destroy his forearms and his cover by using your horizontal elbows.

Elbow Break with the Elbow

This would normally be done after a punch or anything that he sticks his limb out for. Grab the attacker's wrist and slam your elbow/forearm above his elbow as you pull his arm and either breaking or hyper extending his elbow. This is a push/ pull concept.

Side-1

Side-2

TIP:
The power of this move for breaking an elbow is to twist your hips into your strike, using your whole body as well as, pulling his wrist towards you.

Note:
This strike has to be just above the elbow/lower triceps area. My hand is kept on my head to protect myself in case he is still throwing punches.

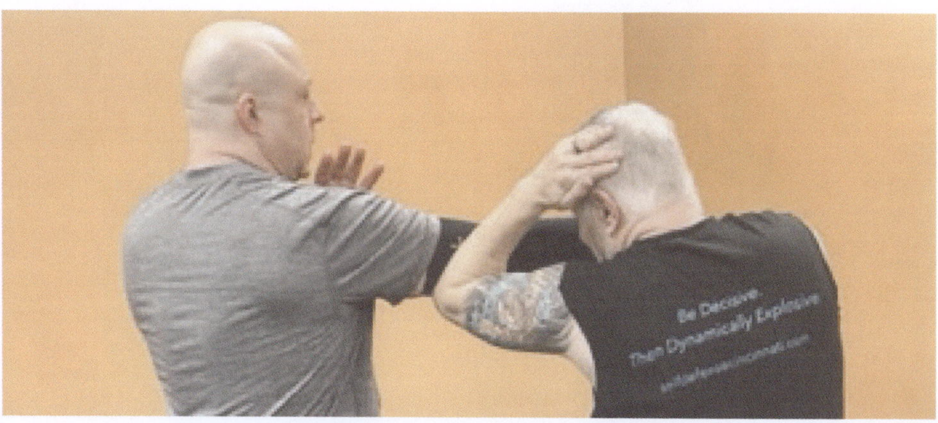

Elbow Break with the Palm

Grab the wrist of the aggressor and pull down as you strike upwards with your palm under the attacker's elbow area at the same time. This is based on the lever principle. Your palm is the fulcrum. This can dislocate the elbow or break it depending how hard you strike and pull down.

Important Details:

The key to making these work is to make sure that the attacker's palm is facing upward, or at least his thumb.

I usually don't go for an elbow break, arm wrench or any kind of joint lock until after I tenderize him. This is because the attacker can fight it. You need to give him something else to think about before hand.

Arm Wrench

An arm wrench can be applied when the attacker leaves his arm out too long and you are able to grab his wrist. The arm wrench works on the lever principle. Your arm should swing upward as if throwing a long uppercut (bolo) above the elbow as the fulcrum point while pulling down violently on his wrist.

Other Elbows

Winged Elbow

This is what I call a "winged elbow" strike. It is a sneaky strike that can follow a spearing elbow. After you impale the attacker with your spearing elbow, wing your arm sideways and use your hips to twist for the power. The hard outer side of your elbow point should make contact with your attacker's jaw or side of their face. This can be followed up with a left horizontal elbow.

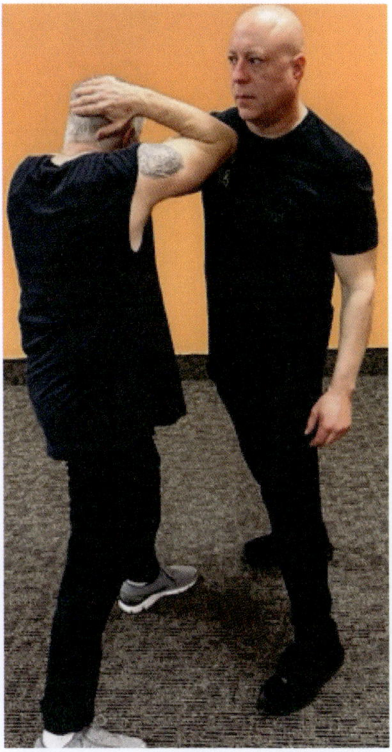

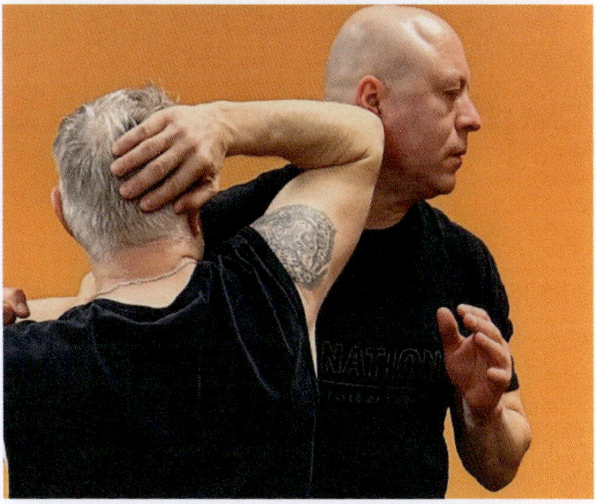

View from behind. Notice the shot right under the ear.

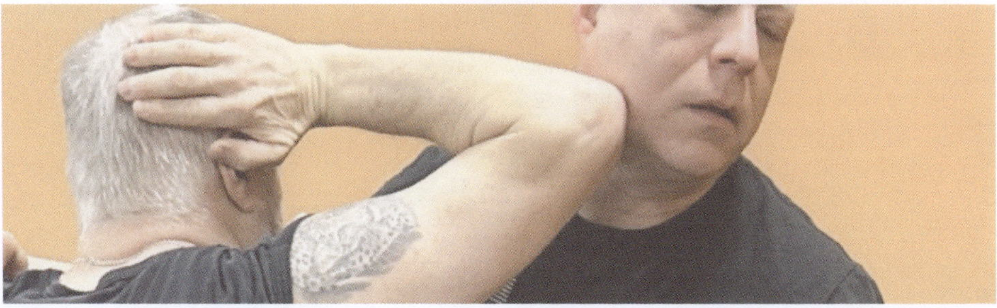

Snap Elbow

A snap elbow is a fast, half beat strike. The elbow snaps out from wherever the arm is (no wind up). Example is to place your hand on someone's chest or shoulder then just snap an elbow to the head. Any direction that you can throw an elbow you can also snap it.

In this scenario I preemptively throw an ear slap at my aggressor. As soon as the slap makes contact with the ear my elbow snaps in on a half beat at his jaw.

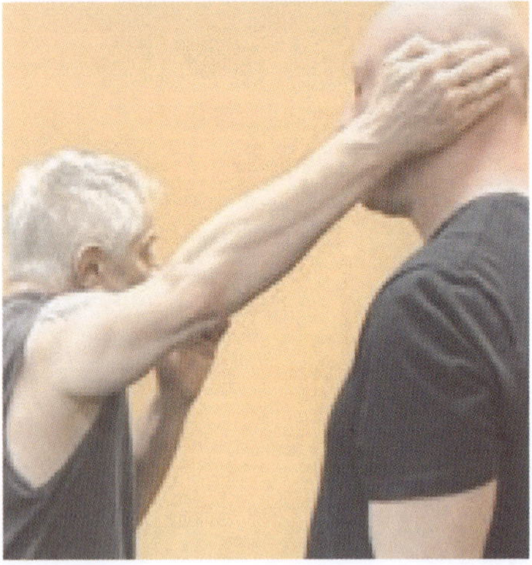

TIP:
The elbow joint must be relaxed and loose in order to snap it

Entries & Sequences Against Attacks

Split Entries

Split entries are great for defending and attacking at the same time. Split means that one arm is on the inside and one arm is on the outside. Notice that the attacker's cross is in between my two arms. I am stepping to the outside of the cross to 11:00 and parrying it with my left hand while my right is attacking his face. The more committed he is with his punch the harder his face is going into my strike. Any strike can be used, a punch (vertical or horizontal), and eye jab, a claw etc. I personally like a "C" strike to the attacker's throat.

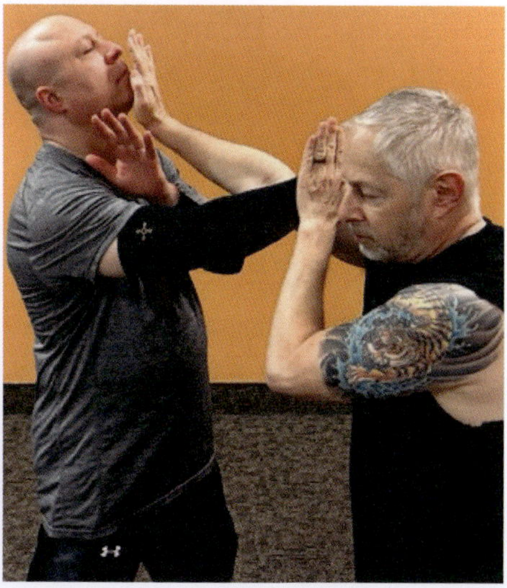

Here the split entry is shown from both sides so you can see how the hands and arms go around the attacker's punching arm.

TIP:
Make sure that when you are executing the split entry your head is off line

Low Line Spit Entry

Step offline to 11:00, your head should move offline about 3"-6" as you parry the cross with your left hand and slap the groin with your right.

Split Entry to Take down

The attacker throws a cross. Step off line and left parry. Throw a inner forearm blade (radial bone) to the left side of his neck. Slap the back of his neck and pull him into his own arm as you do a shoulder shrug and smash his face, Your rear foot goes behind his as you turn, taking him down.

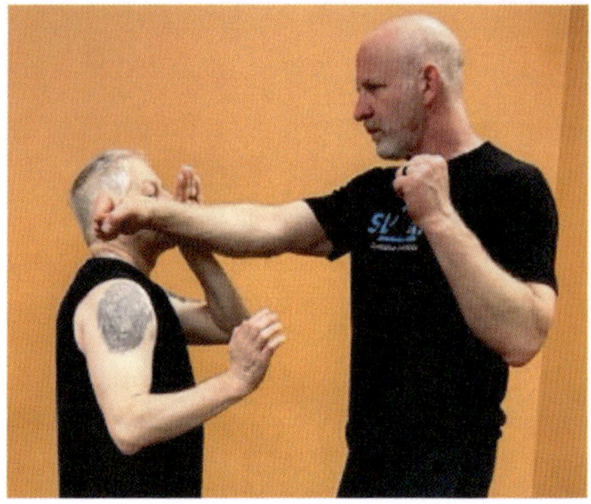

1.

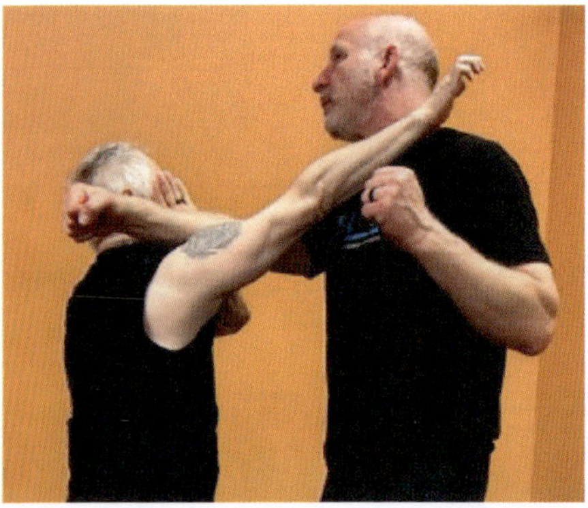

2.

3.

4.

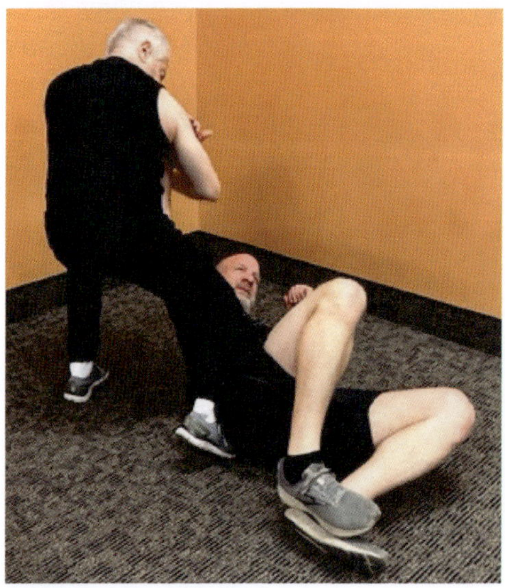

5.

Stop Hits Against Rounded Punches

Shoulder Stop Hit

Biceps Stop Hit

Since a straight punch is faster than a rounded punch. As the punch starts to come shoot a straight palm out to the shoulder of the punch. This will stifle it. I personally like using the biceps stop hit. If you are shorter it is a safer bet. It also hurts the attacker more.

Eye Swipe Against A Straight Punch

As you step off line, parry his jab i this case with your left hand as you come from underneath with a right hand eye swipe. The eye swipe is a crescent motion to the left with the fingers extended and loose.

Note:
If the eye swipe is done correctly and lands it should give you some time for follow-up strikes.

Haymaker Defense 1

One of my favorite sequences that I got from Joe Simonet. Unfortunately, the photos do not do it justice. There are several subtle moves in this sequence that are not shown. The the clavicle drop and the slap are what is known as incidental hits. Note: that I usually will use a supported elbow frame with this sequence, but for the purposes of seeing what my left arm is doing I did not use it.

1 Cover and crash

2 After I crash the left cover arm drops down on the attacker's clavicle.

Note

All through the my sequence I keep my head covered if his punch left comes.

3 I slap/hook the base of the skull and pull the attacker into a diagonal elbow to the face.

Haymaker Defense 2

Another favorite sequence that I got from Joe Simonet. Again cover and crash the haymaker. My left arm over hooks the attacker's punching arm as I grab and dig my fingers around his clavicle bone with my right hand like a suite case handle. My left had grasps my right wrist for support and I violently pull him in toward a head butt, and ripping his clavicle bone from his body or breaking it.

1 Cover and crash

2 Wrap around attacker's punching arm.

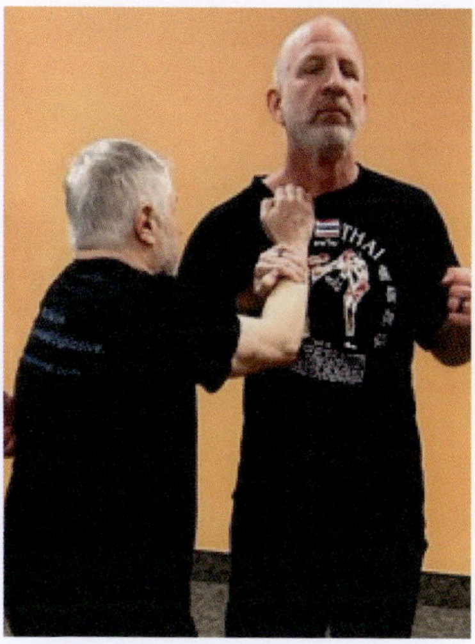

3 I grab and dig around his clavicle bone like I and am holding a suite case handle. The more that I dig my fingers around his bone the more pain he feels.

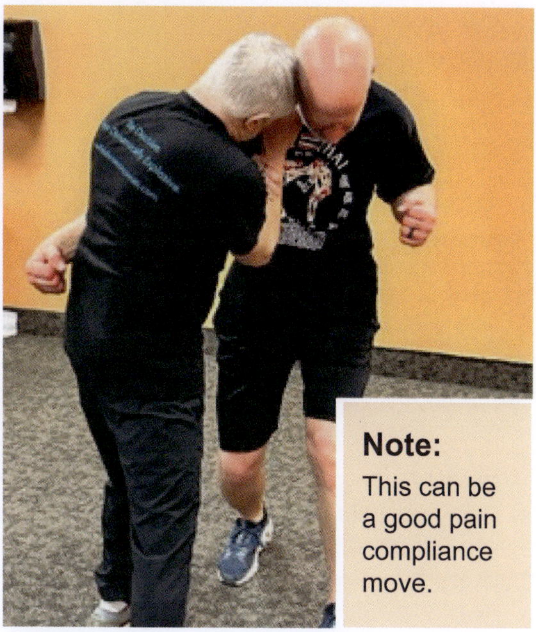

Note:

This can be a good pain compliance move.

4 Violently pull toward my head butt to sepa rate the clavicle from the body.

Shoulder Bump

The shoulder bump is a good way to knock a taller attacker off balance. The key is to quickly drop height (center of gravity) and head straight into the attacker with your shoulder leading like a football player. A hard enough hit could knock the wind out of him.

1 I step off line as I parry the attacker's incoming cross.

2 I quickly drop height and push step off my rear foot and step at an angle into my attacker, leading with my shoulder to his upper ribs.

Continue

My follow up strike will be a reverse hammer fist or a slap to the groin.

Notice:

The way his heel is locked as I hit him. Meaning he is off balance and he will easily fall over.

Deflect Cross into Hammer and Anvil Biceps Destruction

Deflect the cross and slow it down. Grab the wrist with the same hand and pivot. With the other hand palm strike above the elbow area tweaking the arm. Keep your palm where it is and turn your body and drop weight with a right elbow on the biceps. This is called a hammer and anvil because you are holding the body part in place with one hand as you smash it with the other. I usually follow up with a hack to the neck or back fist to the jaw.

1 Step offline with a deflection.

2 Grab the wrist and pivot your body.

3 Upward palm strike above the elbow.

4 Keeping your palm above the elbow, turn and drop weight with an elbow to his biceps.

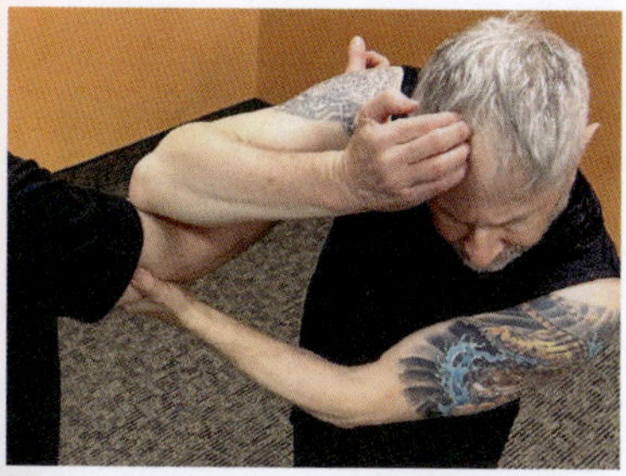

Close up of "Hammer and Anvil" to the biceps.

5 Follow up strikes are a hack to the side of the neck or a back fist to the jaw.

Simple Parry & Punch

As the attacker throws a cross I step off line and parry with my left as I throw a vertical punch of my own to his upper ribs/arm pit area. I stay to the outside to avoid any incoming strikes from his left hand. Under the arm pit is a very good target to strike because there are a network of nerves in the brachial plexus The Axillary nerve is one that when striked can cause a loss of movement, or loss of sensation) and glands that are sensitive.

Vertical punch under arm pit.

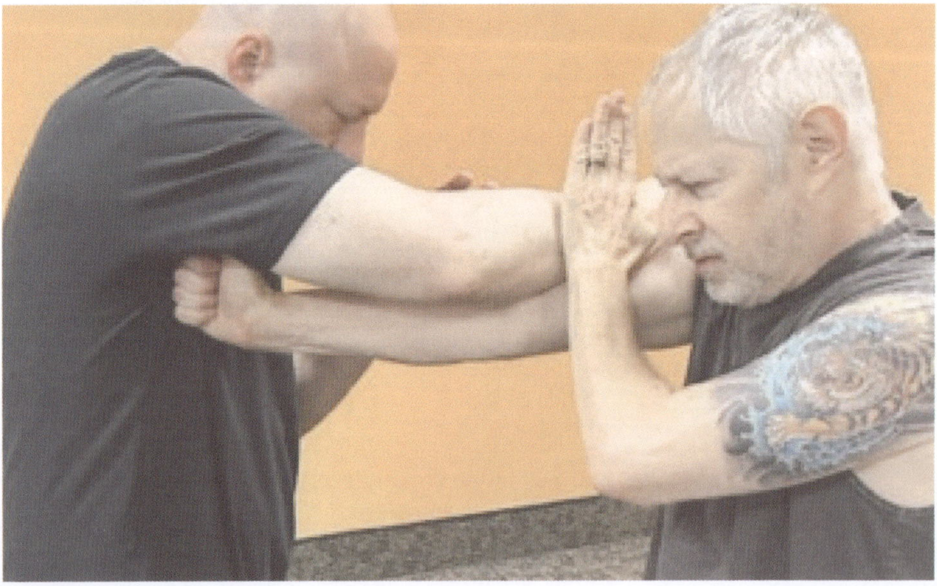

Sequence Against A Jab/Cross using a Reverse Split Entry

This sequence is the opposite of a split entry because of the hands. As the jab comes I scoop it away with my right hand. I use the same right hand to pick up the cross which looks like a high block. My left hand shoots in under my right and under his arm and palm smashes his face. This could also be a vertical fist.

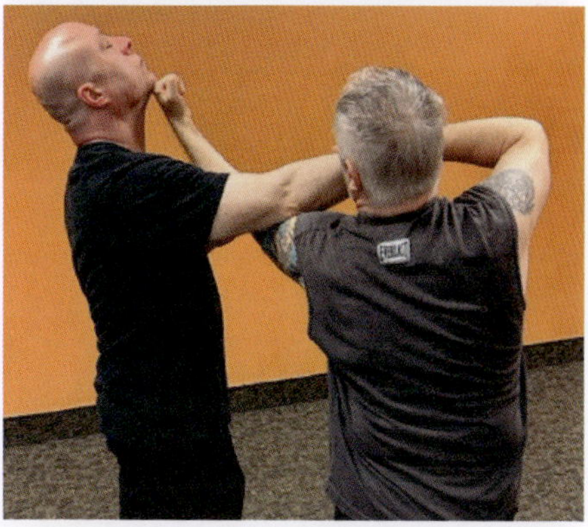

Instead of hitting the face you can throw an uppercut or go low with a shovel hook to the ribs or liver shot.

Sequence Against A Cross

This sequence is a Kenpo move called sleeper. I personally like this move because of the close-line. Instead of trying to put your opponent to sleep, step around his leg with your right foot and take him down.

1 As the cross comes I step off line and parry it.

2 My right arm comes up as I use a close-line to the side of his neck.

Idea:

The close-line strike doesn't have to go to the side of the neck. It can go to the chest or solar plexus and knock the wind out of your aggressor instead.

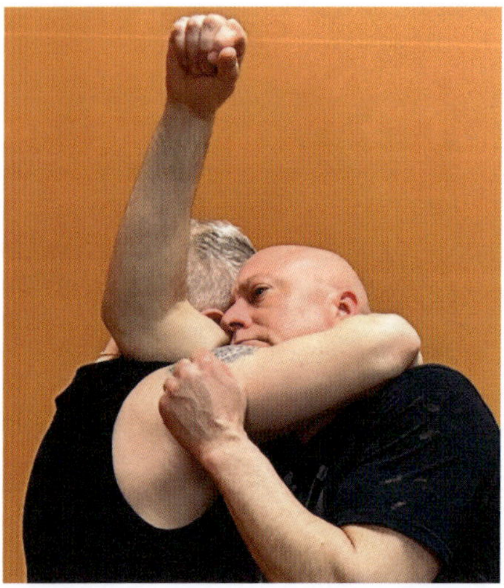

3 I continue to reach around his neck with my right arm as my left arm grabs my wrist putting a choke hold on him. My head pushes sideways into his arm and forces it to push on his carotid artery while my right arm is squeezing the carotid artery on the other side.

Note:

It is hard to put someone to sleep with this hold because getting their arm to push exactly into their carotid artery can be difficult unless you are very strong.
You would have a lot better success with a sleeper if you parried his arm downward and brought the close-line strike over the top of his arm.

I have to mention that the hold itself gives you good control over your opponent because you take his balance.

Sequence Against A Cross Fish Hook

This sequence is a Kenpo move called fish hook. This move's name comes from the angled elbow that comes down on the arm of the jab. I like certain pieces of this sequence. The reverse upward angled hammer fist under the chin is a nice strike that seems to come out of nowhere and is a very hard strike to block.

1 As the jab comes I step off line.

2 My right arm comes up and makes a circular motion downward on the attacker's jabbing arm (Fish Hook).

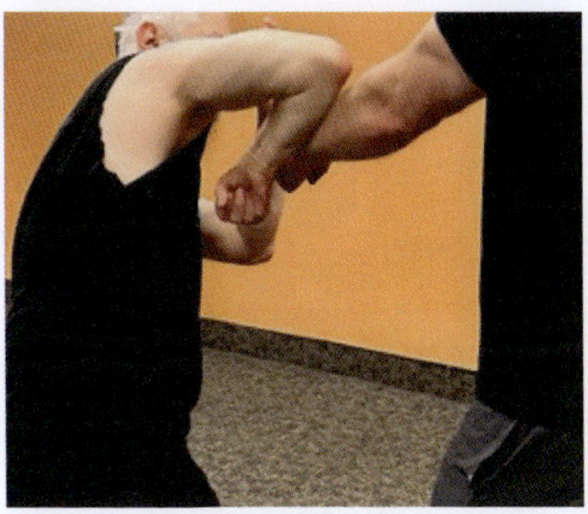

Close up angle of the fish hook from the other side.

3 As the attacker's arm gets elbowed down I use my left hand to monitor and keep it out of the way so I can shoot a reverse upward angled hammer fist under the chin or nose.

Sequence Against Hooks

This sequence is a supported elbow frame cover/crash and a wing cover.

1 As the hook starts I vault and crash into the aggressor using a supported elbow frame cover.

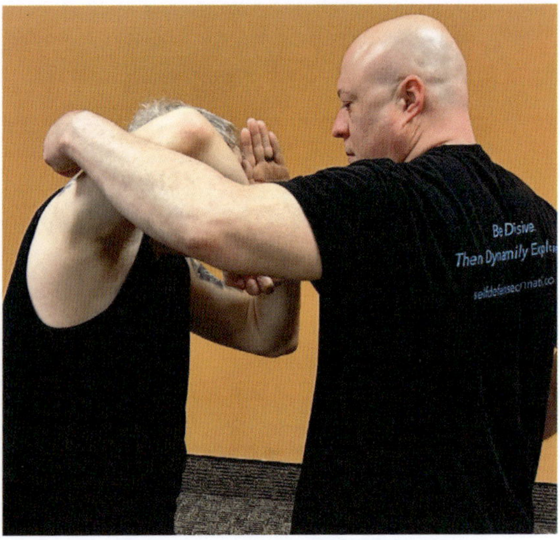

2 As the second hook starts I raise my supporting elbow upward like a wing to cover. Being on the inside of both the aggressor's arms gives me lots of options down the center line.

Notice:
How close this leaves my hands to the aggressor's face.

Sequence Against Hook Cover & Wrap

This sequence is a single cover against a hook and use your cover arm to wrap around his arm that threw the hook.

As the hook starts I step forward and use a single cover. Then I wrap his arm tying it up which is also called an over hook.

Sequence Against A Cross Using Elbows

The attacker throws the jab and I scoop it. As the cross comes I feed it into a horizontal elbow destruction. Immediately after I vault into his space with a supported side elbow to his face, turn and low rear elbow his solar plexus.

1 I scoop the jab and off balance the attacker.

2 Knowing the cross is following I feed it into a horizontal elbow destruction.

Notice:
When elbowing the face I use my other hand/arm to help strike with double the force of impact than a single elbow.

3 As the attacker pulls his fractured hand back, I vault into his space with the point of my supported side elbow into his face.

4 Then I quickly turn and drop weight as I throw a rear elbow to his solar plexus.

Sequence Against Straight Punches (Whirling Leaves)

As the attacker starts throwing a series of straight punches I use a ram's horn cover. I then time his punches and explode slapping each punch down and back knuckling the aggressor's face. The ending (Whirling Leaves) comes from chinese Kenpo.

1 As the attacker throws a series of aggressive straight punches I use a ram's horn to cover up.

2 As I keep covered, I time the punches when the aggressor's left punch hit my right forearm I do what is known as a smother block which is slapping his punch down.

3 As the right punch comes the I smother that down with my left hand as my right hand back knuckles his face. The whole sequence is a fast circular (whirling) arm movement.

TIP:

Timing and sensitivity are key to making this work. Also constant forward pressure while slapping the fists down adds to the explosiveness.

Picture your hands rolling forward, right then left and right again.

Grappling

This book's focus is not about grappling, but I have to talk a little on the subject because it pertains to dirty boxing.

Base, Angle, Leverage

You need **at least two out of the three** of these to control the grappling/clinching range. Especially for throwing, sweeping an opponent or keeping them off balance.

Dumog (Arm Choke Point)

In Dumog they use a choke point, the upper arm to move an opponent. One hand grabs the biceps and the other the triceps of the opponent's arm, lift upward and push or pull. You will be amazed that you can move a person considerably larger and heavier than yourself. This works because you are lifting the bigger person's hips above their center of gravity, which disrupts their base. Keeping your knees slightly bent and hips lowered will help your center of gravity (base). Bruce Lee use to do a trick like this. However, this really isn't a trick. It is physics, and it is very useful if you need to man handle a larger aggressive person.

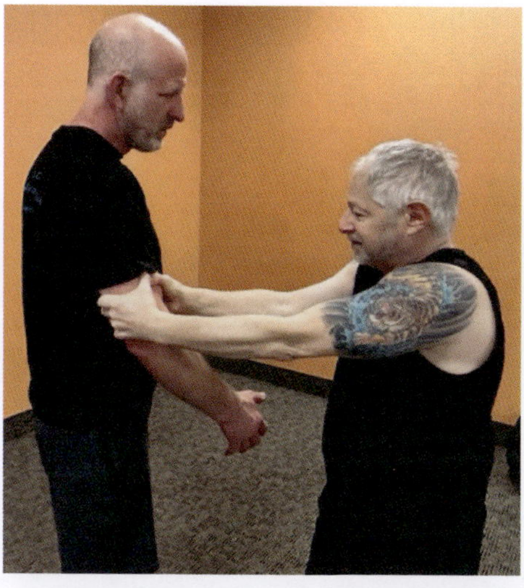

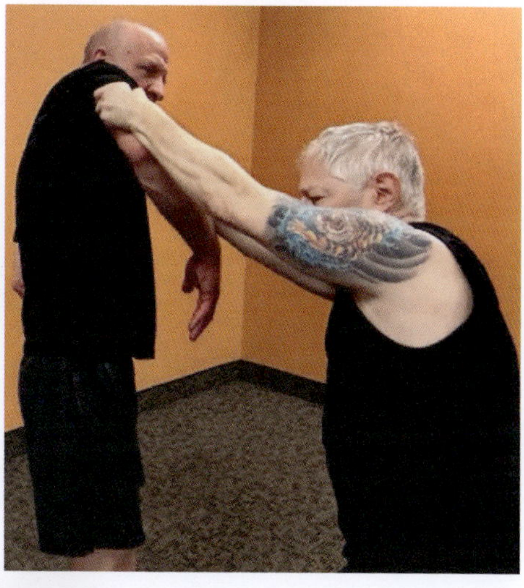

Striking from the Clinch

Striking from the clinch can be challenging because the reason that you clinched in the first place is that your attacker does not want to get hit, but rather use his strength to over power you and take you to the ground. The key to being able to strike from the clinch is to make some space to work, and keeping your aggressor off balance. **Caution:** Do NOT make too much space. If you give a good wrestler some space, be prepared to go to the ground. That is where you will wind up!

TIP: Since the high line is tied up, the best bet is to attack the low line and tenderize to take your aggressor's attention off the high line.

Old School Dirty Boxing Clinch Sequence

I got this from Kelly McCann. Back when gloves had laces a boxer would use the laces part of the glove to rub across his opponent's face to irritate him in the clinch. This is where this sequence comes from. Since we don't have gloves on the street I use the palm of my right hand to hit and turn the attacker's face which also makes some distance as well. I immediately use the blade (ulnar bone) of my left forearm to hack into the side of his neck and create a frame. Once I startle him and get more space between us I use hammer fists or control him.

1 From the clinch I try to have at least one of my arms on the inside of his.

2 I take my right hand and palm the side of his face which turns it and gives me some space.

3 I slam my left forearm into the side of his neck creating a frame.

4 Now my right hand is free to throw strike s.

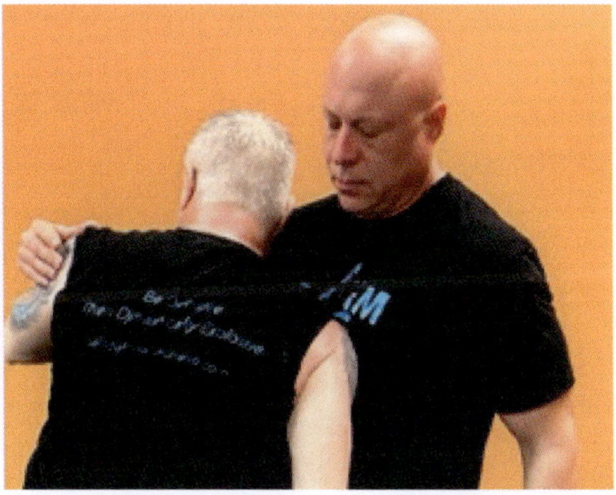

Shoulder Bump

A shoulder bump is used to throw your opponent off balance and make space to strike.

Shoulder Shrug

A shoulder shrug is a good strike when you attacker's head is close to you. The shoulder goes up hitting under his chin.

Note:
The side that is bumping or shrugging has to have the arm on the inside of the clinch.

Side Head Butt

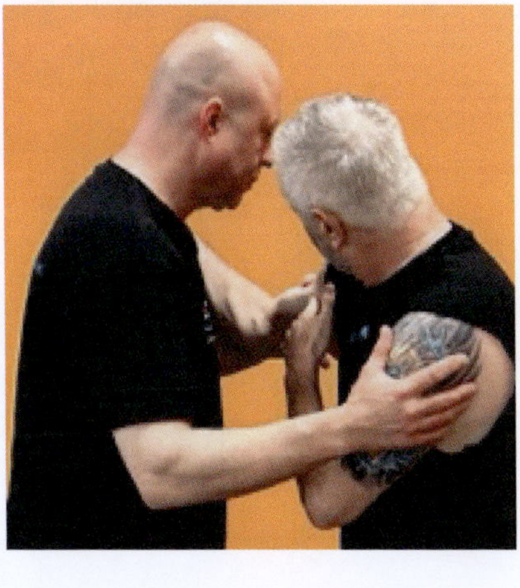

Biceps or Forearm Pop Out

A pop out is a strike that is used to get space. To get the pop out either slap or grab the back of you attacker's neck, pulling him in hard and fast. Loosen your elbow and shoot your arm out while twisting it into the side of his neck or jaw. When done correctly his head should shoot back and you will need to catch it by hooking you hand or he will be out of reach for the next strike.

Cross Face Forearm Strike

A cross face forearm strike is great from keeping a larger attacker from grabbing or bear hugging you. This works on the elbow frame concept. It is strong and won't collapse. I personally like it because it turns your attacker's face away. A good follow up is an under hook to a shoulder lock and a knee to the face.

Getting Out of the Thai Clinch

The Thai Clinch from Thai boxing is one of the roughest clinches to get out of if your opponent know how to properly do it.

1 My opponent has me in a tight Thai clinch.

2 I automatically throw my hands up under his chin and push up and back to get him off balance. If he is off balance, he does not have a good base to keep me clinched up.

Note:
This is basically a supported chin jab strike.

3 As I get the attacker's head and upper body to go back, his lower half of his body comes forward. That is when I knee Mr. Groin.

Double Biceps Tie

The double biceps tie lets you control both of the attacker's arms so that he can not strike. However, note while you are holding his arms you can not strike either. This is just used as a brief control point. Below is one scenario that could be used off the double biceps tie up.

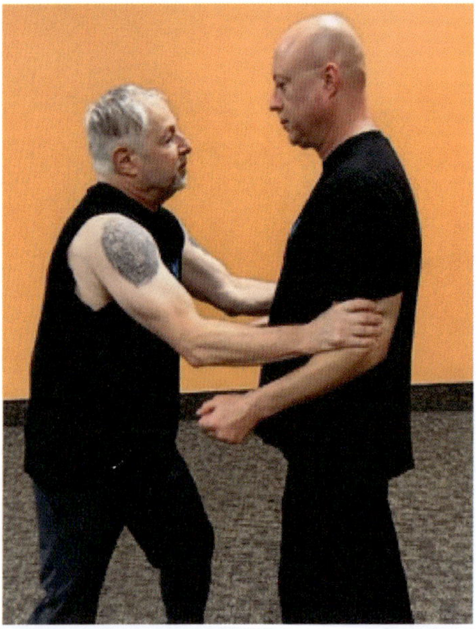

1 I have control of both my opponent's arms so that he can not strike me.

2 I violently spin him clockwise so that he is no longer facing me. This way when I let go I do not have to deal with all his weapons.

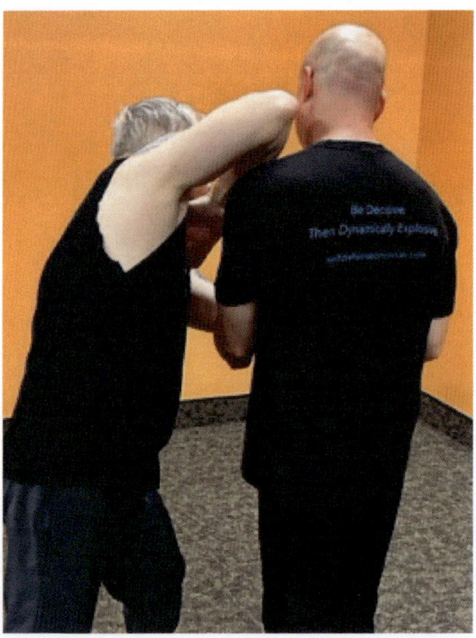

3 I let go of his arm with my right and quickly throw an elbow at his jaw.

Notice:
Since I turned him and with the angle that I have he never even sees the elbow coming.

Ending Sequences Continuous Follow Ups

Cycling Hammer Fists

This is a primal follow-up that will overwhelming your attacker. Nothing feels more primal than smashing hammer fists into something or someone. This is also very explosive, with forward pressure that keeps your opponent going backward on his heels. The target is the bridge of the nose. The goal is to smash his nose flat into his face. The cycling is done by making fast large circles with your shoulders and coming down with your hammer fists one after the other. Your feet are shuffling forward taking up his space with each strike.

Cycling Hammer Fist Sequence

Straight Blast (Chain Punching)

The straight blast comes from Wing Chun Kung Fu and Bruce Lee's Jeet Kune Do. Vertical punches, both fists perpendicularly above one another that cycle in a forward circular motion one after the other. This is an awesome way to overwhelm your attacker and make him back pedal on the heels of his feet. Each arm's movement is like a trains' coupling rod that goes back and forth. One fist goes out, the other goes back in. As you are doing this with your arms/fists your feet are doing the 50 yard dash down your opponent's center line. This is all about forward pressure.

Straight Blast Sequence

Head butts, Knees and Elbows

Paul Vunak coined the term "**Head Butts, Knees and Elbows**." Once you get through No Mans' Land and enter into clinching range, start to incorporate any combination of head butts, knees and elbows. Throw non-stop, continuous diagonal elbows, horizontal elbows, vertical elbows, knees, and head butts in any order which I call the ***"Blender of Pain". Every time you touch him, hurt him!***

Incidental striking are hits that are not planned, but happen to be available if they are there on the way to another strike do it.

Vertical Elbow under the Chin

Incidental Striking:
Every time you touch a guy, Hurt him!
– Kelly McCann

Clearing Obstructions

Clearing an Obstruction 1

This is a way to get out of that clustered entanglement which is basically a stalemate. It also avoids the clinching and grappling.

Pak Sao Da (Slapping Hand with Vertical Punch)

This is a Wing Chun term for slapping the obstruction out of the way and continuing with the attack. In this scenario we both have our guard up and have crashed. **1**. This is a stalemate position. His arm is an obstruction in my way that I have to remove if I want to continue and get the upper hand. **2**. With my free hand I slap down on his forearm with explosive forward pressure so that his arm goes against his body. **3**. Now that I have his arm (the obstruction) out of my way I can continue to attack with a vertical fist to the side of his face.

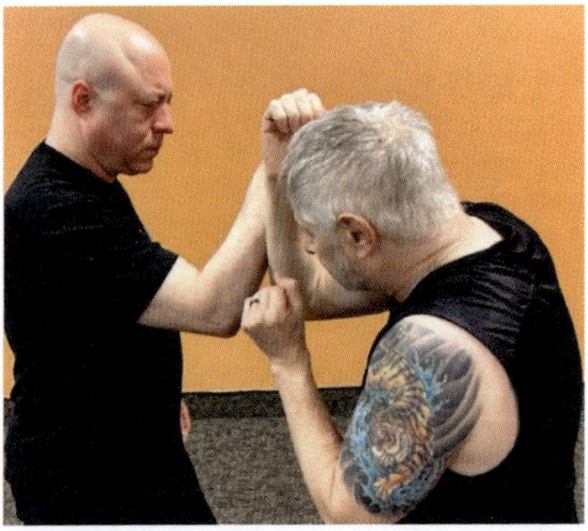

1. Stalemate position. Our arms are in each others way.

2. I quickly Pak Sao his forearm out of my way.

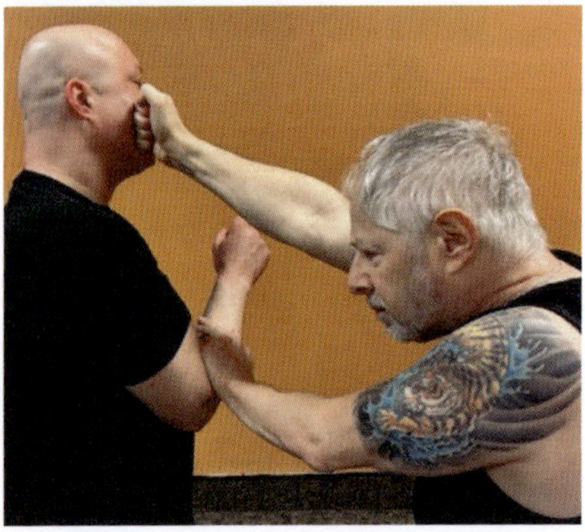

3. I am now free to follow up with a vertical fist to his face.

Follow Up:
A good follow up after this is a straight blast (chain punching).

Kina Mutai or Kina Motay

Unconventional Tactics

This is a primal tactics for when the shit hits the fan. Bites, rips, twists, gouges and tears. No such thing as political correctness in the street when fighting for your life.

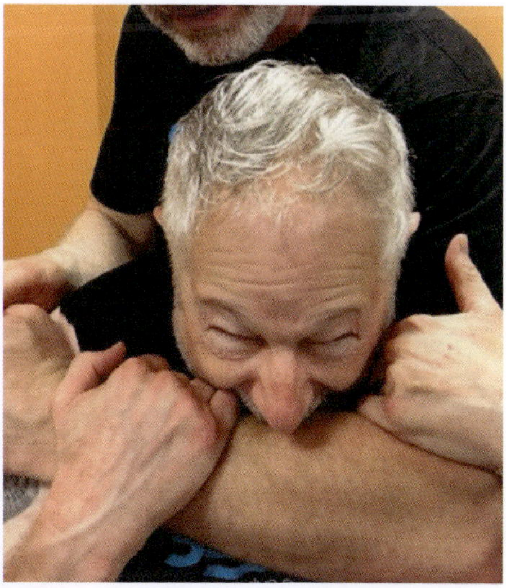

Bite

To get out of a strong hold.

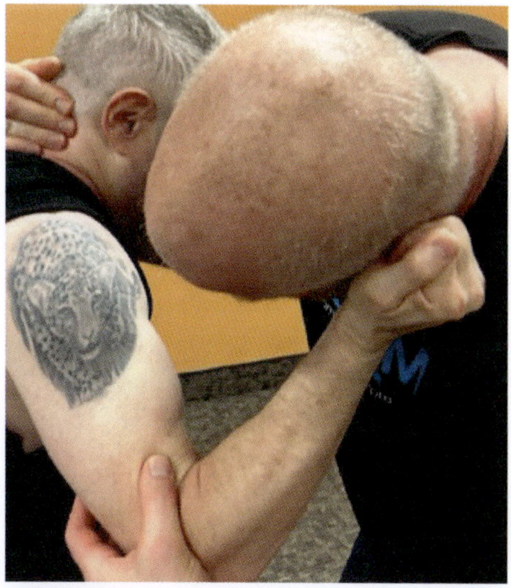

Ear Rip

Grab the his ear and rip downward.

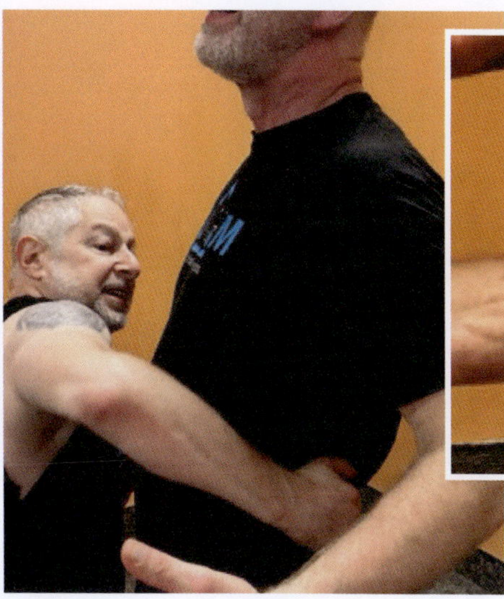

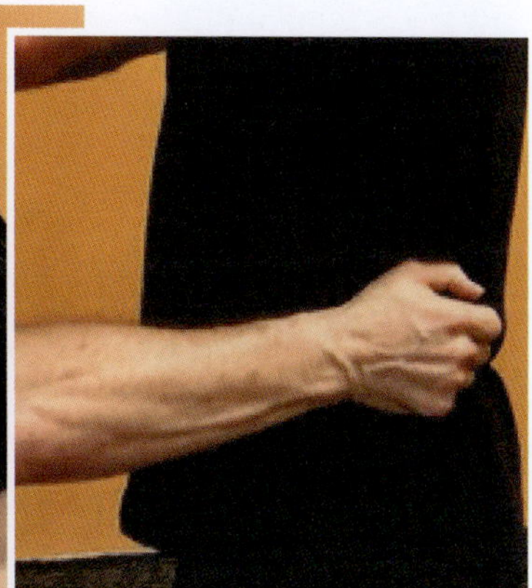

Twist

Grab a hand full of his (fat) or extra skin while digging in with your nails on his side or back and twist until he screams, then twist more.

All these "unconventional" tactics can be done on any parts of the body, especially where there is loose fat or skin.

Training

The goal when training is to try and get as comfortable as possible mentally and physically under stressful situations. Drills should amp up the adrenaline rush as close as possible to a real confrontation. Of course, we can only take this so far. Most likely we are training in a nice facility, and we know everyone in the class so there are always limitations vs the real encounter on the street. The most fearsome part on the street is not knowing.

Realistic drills and scenarios. The attacker should be aggressively animated with his movements and use vocal aggression, cursing etc.

When physical use resistance. Don't give in because your partner is supposed to win. Make it feel like a real fight.

Less is More..

"I fear not the man who has practiced 10,000 kicks once, but I fear the man who has practiced one kick 10,000 times."

- Bruce Lee

I offer a lot of sequences and ideas in this book. The goal is not to try and use all of them. Train and try different ones until you come up with only a handful that you feel comfortable and confident with. Then work them until they become muscle memory and second nature. We are going for quality, not quantity.

This is the problem with too many martial arts systems. There are literally so many techniques that when faced with a situation you hesitate because you don't know what to choose. If you haven't heard of the OODA Loop, look this up and you will know what I am talking about.

Train with Intensity

Mind-set:

Mushin
The ultimate goal is to not memorize techniques, but have things ingrained in your subconscious and just come out without thinking? The Japanese call it "Mushin" meaning no mind.

If you have to stop and think about what you are going to do, you are already behind.

There is no substitute for training.
If you don't' train, you won't hone your skills. You need to train with resistance, making it as realistic as possible within reason. Part of training is learning how to deal with the chaos when you are in the storm. That is what a fight is...**chaos**, when two bodies collide and start throwing limbs at each other. It is not pretty like portrayed in the movies.

USA

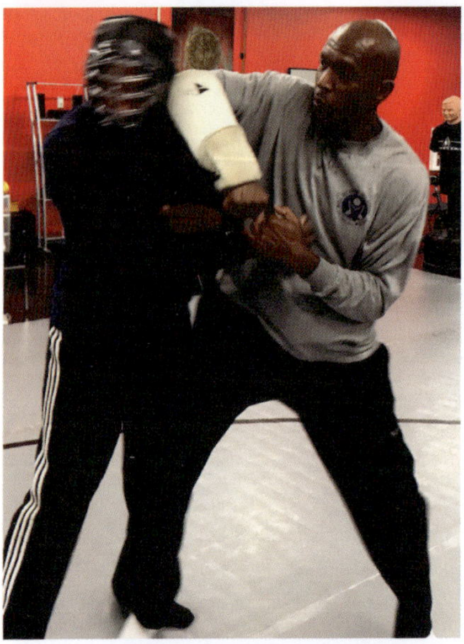

BOON

nspiration

Printed in Dunstable, United Kingdom

81641708R00054